beth levine shoes

beth levine shoes

HELENE VERIN

Introduction by HAROLD KODA

Stewart, Tabori & Chang   New York

Published in 2009 by
Stewart, Tabori & Chang, an imprint of Harry N. Abrams, Inc.

Text copyright © 2009 by Helene Verin
Introduction © 2009 by Harold Koda
Foreword © 2009 by Sonja Bata, O.C.

All photographs, unless otherwise noted, copyright © 2009 by David Hamsley

The photograph on page 34 has been previously copyrighted by Milton H. Greene © 2009 Joshua Greene All Rights Reserved.
Pages 2–3: *Tuxedo*, 1956. Tricolor silk satin pump with bow.
Pages 6–7: Title unknown, circa 1970. Suede with silver kidskin woven strips over wedge.

Library of Congress Cataloging-in-Publication Data
Verin, Helene.
  Beth Levine shoes / Helene Verin.
     p. cm.
  Includes bibliographical references.
  ISBN 978-1-58479-759-3
  1. Shoes--United States--Design. 2. Shoes--United States--Pictorial
works. 3. Levine, Beth, 1914-2006. 4. Herbert Levine, Inc. I. Title.
  TT678.5.V47 2008
  685'.310092--dc22

                    2008037918

Editor: Rahel Lerner
Designer: Alissa Faden
Production Manager: Tina Cameron

The text of this book was composed in Didot and Chalet

Printed in China
10 9 8 7 6 5 4 3 2 1

HNA ▩▩▩▩
harry n. abrams, inc.
a subsidiary of La Martinière Groupe
115 West 18th Street
New York, NY 10011
www.hnabooks.com

To my mother, Bea
and my mentor, Beth

contents

Preface

Beth walks into the living room of her Greenwich Village apartment wearing a black and white polka dot crisp cotton shirt, black and white bandana on her head, completed by black and white houndstooth slippers. "Did you see this article? Women are buying sandals that don't fit, their toes encased in Band-Aids! What's wrong with these shoe manufacturers? Haven't they learned anything?" She pours herself a scotch and stares at the sheep grazing in a meadow (a Milton Avery painting) over the fireplace. "If a shoe is beautiful but doesn't fit the foot, it's not a quality shoe. The woman who wears me knows me intimately . . . if it hurts her, it hurts me."

Americans historically have looked up to European fashion designers for innovation, quality, and advanced fashion. Yet, one of the most original and ingenious shoe designers was a quintessential American, Beth Levine, whose shoes were manufactured in New York City. Her inventive creations are legendary and changed the footwear world forever.

Although Beth had no formal training in shoe design, she became one of the most outstanding fashion designers of the twentieth century. Her unique designs had whimsy and brilliance that no one has ever matched. She didn't bother doing anything in life unless she found it "amusing" and "worthwhile."

I first met Beth when I came to New York in the late 1970s as a struggling shoe designer. She was my mentor, idol, and friend for twenty-five years. Beth's vitality and spunk are evident not only in her designs but also in her remarkable no-holds-barred personality. Each story she told revealed how the daughter of Patchogue farmers became one of the twentieth century's great designers.

Beth, a one-time thoroughbred owner and lifetime bettor, won the triple on the Preakness after selecting the winning Derby horse because it was her lucky color—gray. Going to the local OTB to collect the winnings on her $1 bet, she smiled knowingly and said, "You've got to trust your instincts." Thank goodness Beth trusted hers for over nine decades.

Helene Verin
Fall 2008

Beth Levine.

Foreword

SONJA BATA, O.C.
FOUNDER AND CHAIRMAN, THE BATA SHOE MUSEUM

There are few people who have had a greater influence on me than Beth Levine. We both shared a life-long passion for shoes, for different reasons and in very different ways.

My dream as a young girl was to be an architect, but I fell in love with a shoe man and as a result became deeply absorbed in the footwear industry. I loved good design but needed help to understand fashion trends.

Beth always loved shoes and had a flair for trends. She herself had perfect small feet and her career started as a shoe model for Herbert Levine. Beth married Herbert in 1946, which is the same year I married my husband Thomas and became involved in the Bata Shoe Organization. Herbert and Beth Levine were the perfect couple. He was the businessman, she was his muse.

I am not certain when Beth and I met for the first time, but it was probably in the early 1950s, when I traveled regularly from Europe to America to attend meetings of the American footwear industry. From the European point of view, America at that time was particularly admired and imitated for its casual footwear, such as loafers and saddle oxfords, but less so for dress shoes. There were very few American shoe designers inspiring international fashion. The latest shoe fashion trends came from Europe, where the Dior "New Look" silhouette, with narrow waists and longer feminine skirts, had revolutionized footwear fashion as well. After the war, women were keen to become more feminine again; they wanted high heels and pointed toes with their new outfits.

Herbert Levine always made beautiful shoes, but it was in the 1950s, when Beth Levine launched her elegant stretch boots, that the Levine name became internationally known. Beth succeeded in taking boots out of the protective winter gear category by designing them as fashion statements. Her tight-fitting boots were so incredibly sexy that they very quickly made an impact worldwide.

Her exuberance had no limits. She was truly passionate about her profession. She loved shoes, had wonderful taste, and was able to recognize trends in their earliest stages. She also was an innovator who always dared to experiment with radically new shapes and materials, such as acrylic for heels and clear vinyl uppers. Some of her designs were very elegant; others were just pure fun like her car shoes, her paper shoes, and her grass sandal. To amuse her husband, she even created what she called "silly innovations," like the "No-Shoe."

Beth did not waver in her judgment. She had strong opinions and a tremendous gift for identifying details that would give special flair to a shoe and make it uniquely elegant.

When I started thinking about The Bata Shoe Museum in the late 1980s, I often spoke with Beth. She knew so much about American footwear fashion, and it was a pleasure to listen to her because she spoke with such enthusiasm. She knew her facts but always interlinked them with an array of amusing little personal stories. She had a tremendous memory for everything having to do with shoes—who launched which style in which month, and so on. She was a walking encyclopedia of twentieth-century shoe fashion because she cared so much. It was her life.

Having lunch with Beth in New York was always an enormous treat. There was so much to talk and laugh about. She could sometimes be critical of her competitors or her customers, but always in a humorous way.

We became friends. Beth was intrigued by the idea of a shoe museum and had very definite ideas on what was appropriate and what was not. When I suggested organizing a retrospective exhibition of her work in The Bata Shoe Museum in Toronto in 1999, she was delighted and immediately became involved in all aspects of planning and implementation. The exhibition was entitled "Herbert and Beth Levine: An American Pair." She chose Michael Vollbracht as exhibit designer because she trusted his judgment, and they collaborated on many of the details. Her taste was exquisite and contributed greatly to the success of the exhibition.

Beth never appeared to grow old. When she was well over eighty she still inspired young people with her panoply of stories, all based on personal experience, about the people she had known and the colleagues with whom she had worked. She enjoyed the company of young people and was always ready to be their mentor.

Many of us will remember her with the greatest affection. Beth Levine will remain an inspiration to shoe people all around the world.

Introduction

HAROLD KODA, CURATOR-IN-CHARGE OF THE COSTUME
INSTITUTE AT THE METROPOLITAN MUSEUM OF ART

In 1976, one year after they closed their business, Herbert and Beth Levine were celebrated with a retrospective of their work by The Costume Institute at The Metropolitan Museum of Art. For over three decades, Beth had originated the collections of her husband's eponymous label and established the cutting edge of shoe design in America. Curated by the Levines' longtime friend, former Neiman Marcus executive Arthur Englander, dozens of examples of Beth's innovative creations were arranged on pedestals or, to better emphasize their profiles, mounted in groupings on walls.

For the installation of the exhibition, Beth lent Englander the honey-colored leather cobbler's apron that she used to wear in her studio. This deceptively prosaic garment (it was in fact made by Hermès) was quintessentially Beth. In its utility it reflected the designer's hands-on involvement in the crafting of her shoes, while in its simple luxury it revealed her insistence on chic—even in the down-and-dirty, glue-and-hobnails process entailed in working out her designs.

Unfortunately, no catalogue of the exhibition exists. However, many of the pieces selected by Englander were eventually donated to the permanent archives of the museum. These shoes and boots represent some of Beth's wildest experiments: driving pumps in the form of cars, slides lined in AstroTurf, or stocking boots that extended into a wrapped bodysuit. Although she prided herself on her pragmatism—inventing, for example, a spring mechanism for the insteps of her mules to prevent them from slipping off—Beth's imagination was much too expansive to be fettered by mere functionalism. Her signature designs are poised between the realms of utility and aesthetics, comfort and seduction. Beth's great talent was to explore a variety of stylistic themes—postwar modernism, orientalist exoticism, space-age utopianism, pop-art whimsy—and inflect them all with a clearly American idiom.

As with many designers whose careers began in the period immediately following World War II, Beth's innovations, while familiar to fashion specialists and her surviving contemporaries, are less well known to the wider public of today. Over the years, Beth's signature designs have been sought after by private collectors and museums and have continued to influence designers. When Tokio Kumagai showed a line of playfully appliquéd flats in his Place des Victoires boutique in the 1980s, they were immediately recognizable as the progeny of Beth's pop art–inspired work of twenty years earlier. More recently, when the buckled pilgrim shoe made famous by Roger Vivier was revived, few knew that it was a style first proposed by Beth and originally taken up by the French designer only at the urging of American buyers.

It is time to give credit where credit is due. In an era when American fashion was still in the shadow of Parisian haute couture, Beth's work achieved international prominence. While fashion designers such as Claire McCardell and Bonnie Cashin established an American vocabulary of sportswear distinct from European models, Beth's sensibility never rejected the sophistication of postwar high fashion. Instead, she was able to inject a fresh clarity and modernity into the prevailing notions of elegance. Diana Vreeland, the iconic editor of *Harper's Bazaar* and *Vogue*, determined that Beth's American designs transcended even Vreeland's highest Francophilic standards. Happily, Beth's career and designs were well documented in her own time and are reinforced by records and scrapbooks from the designer's own archives. Of course, her wry reminiscences and lively anecdotal repartee provide a perfect framework for the rich history of her contributions to twentieth-century shoe design.

The Costume Institute collection includes an example of Beth's minimalist, "topless" shoe, consisting only of an arched sole of a shoe attached to a narrow high heel. Beth intended that it be worn by means of adhesive pads joining the shoe to the foot. The black silk edge of the sole outlining the foot and the stem-like heel are barely visible. Essentially, the effect is of a bared, tiptoeing foot: nature supported by artifice. Like much of Beth's work, it embodies elegance achieved through material mastery, aesthetic virtuosity, and ironic wit: pure Herbert Levine, and pure Beth.

HER LIFE

early years

Elizabeth "Bessie" Katz was born in Patchogue, Long Island on December 31, 1914. She was the third of five children born to Israel Katz and Anna Cohen, both of whom came from Rokiskis, a village in Lithuania. When he was twenty-five years old, Israel Katz rode on a horse from New York City to eastern Long Island, where he set up a cattle and dairy farm in Holtsville. Beth referred to herself as a "farmer's daughter" and cherished her childhood. She grew up surrounded by animals, vegetable gardens, pastures, and the ocean. She adored horses and riding boots, and as a young child she already knew the difference between calfskin, kidskin, cowhide, and sheepskin.

The family didn't have much money, and her mother sewed all the clothes for her five children. But the one thing Anna Katz couldn't make, and on which she insisted on sparing no expense, was footwear.

Growing up among Jewish and Italian immigrants on Long Island, Bessie had opportunities to exhibit her unique brand of creativity in cooking as well as taking care of the farm. Food was always an important part of Bessie's life; her mother churned butter and made noodles, her father set up a butcher shop in the back and sold chickens, eggs, and beef. Her father and her brother Abe would have semiannual pickle contests to determine who made the best dill pickles in the family. Abe was the practical joker of the family, and he once spelled his initials on the front lawn using a bucket of cow blood. One of Bessie's chores was cutting the grass and the blood had an extraordinary amount of nitrogen in it, so she was furious that she now had to tend the overfertilized grass three

Bessie Katz on her horse, circa 1917.

times a week instead of the normal once. Although her father stood five feet two inches, he was a powerful presence, forbidding Abe to marry his non-Jewish sweetheart. (Abe never married.)

The Katz parents kept kosher and spoke Yiddish in their home at 25 West Avenue in Patchogue. It was a two-family house and the upstairs was rented out. The seven members of the Katz family shared two bedrooms and one bathroom. Bessie and her siblings attended public schools in Patchogue, all of them graduating from Patchogue High School.

Above left: Beth and her father, Israel Katz, circa 1940. Above right: Beth at Holtsville farm, date unknown. Below (clockwise from top left): Beth, Israel ("Pop"), Sara, Ruth, Abe, and Zelda Katz, circa 1945.

Anna Katz (middle), Beth (right, on elbows), circa 1920.

In 1938, Bessie, now called Beth, followed her older sister Sara to New York City, with the intention of enrolling in the Pratt Institute to become a social worker, but she needed a job to support herself. At that time, the highest-quality shoes in the world were manufactured in the United States, with factories concentrated in downtown New York and Brooklyn. From the 1920s to the 1950s, "Made in Brooklyn" and "New York Shoes" denoted luxury and craftsmanship. Having been blessed with sample-size feet (4B), Beth responded to an advertisement for a secretary and shoe model. The manufacturer was Palter DeLiso, a high-grade shoe manufacturer in New York City. Vincent DeLiso, one of the company's partners and a respected and creative designer, encouraged Beth's imagination and learned to respect her judgment. Beth would try on shoes for customers, and it soon became clear that she had taste, stamina, and an intuitive feel for how a shoe fit and what made it comfortable or not. "I could tell anything from the inside of the shoe. I could even tell by the feel of the shoe how it had been manufactured."[1] Beth regarded her feet as a tool, much as hands are to a potter.

While working at Palter DeLiso, Beth tried on the first open-toed shoes for daywear, considered déclassé in the 1930s. Dan Palter, also a partner at the company, invited

Mrs. Edna Woolman Chase, editor in chief of *Vogue* magazine, to the showroom to see these revolutionary shoes. Model Beth was embarrassed, feeling undressed in front of the formidable Mrs. Chase. In the next issue of *Vogue*, Chase declared open-toed shoes "in bad taste." Palter had already sold them to every one of his accounts—and each account called to cancel. He begged them to take the shoes and offered to take them back if they didn't sell. They all sold. Mrs. Chase admitted in her book *Always in Vogue* that the only mistake in her career was being wrong about open-toed shoes for daywear.[2] Beth worked at Palter DeLiso for four years, absorbing knowledge about fit, style, and what it took to make quality footwear.

She then moved to I. Miller, which was the largest quality manufacturer at the time. There were no "designers" there, but rather "line builders," known as "knock-off artists." Europe—France in particular—was considered the provenance of *haute couture*, and American designers were expected to sketch and produce copies of European designs. Beth worked in the sample department, writing specification sheets as well as modeling. Women were not welcome in the shoe industry on the whole, and Beth quickly realized that her insights and ideas were routinely ignored. She left I. Miller and did stints at the Carlisle Shoe Company and Pincus-Tobias, both high-grade shoe factories in lower Manhattan. During that period, she came into contact with retailers, manufacturers, and salesmen who would prove invaluable in the coming years.

With the coming of World War II, Beth felt that there were more important things to be doing with her life than designing beautiful shoes, so she resigned from the business and joined the American Red Cross. (Many of her friends in France continued to call her by the nickname "Croix Rouge" until the end of her life.) She was stationed at Halloran General Hospital in Staten Island, where she organized recreational and entertainment programs for wounded veterans. On weekends, she would bring injured soldiers to her family's farm in Patchogue to recuperate.

When the war ended, she wasn't sure if she wanted to return to the male chauvinistic shoe business. Women were a rarity in the factories and there were no female retailers, salespeople, accountants, lawyers, or executives in the industry. Because of her sample-size feet, the salesmen would have her model the shoes but her comments were not welcome. The factory workers would roll their eyes and resist new concepts. Although there were a few women shoe designers (Mabel Julianelli and Margaret Clark, for instance), they were poorly paid and treated with far less respect than their male colleagues. All questions about manufacturing, sales, distribution, and advertising would be directed to men, with the few "girls" having responsibility only for color and trim.

* * *

While Beth was growing up on the farm on Long Island, her future husband and partner, Herbert Levine, was growing up nearby in the Bronx. Herbert was born April 19, 1916, at 926 Southern Boulevard. His father, Samuel Eli Levine, and mother, Bessie Edson, were in the cigar business and enjoyed their most prosperous years during the Depression.

Herbert was a brilliant, debonair man who graduated magna cum laude and Phi Beta Kappa from Dartmouth College in 1937. It was unusual for a Jewish boy to find himself in a town like Hanover, New Hampshire, in the 1930s, but Herb got in to Dartmouth thanks to the 5 percent Jewish quota that had to be filled. In college, he worked at the student newspaper, the *Daily Dartmouth,* becoming the editorial head by his senior year. Having been drawn to theater ever since seeing his first Broadway show in 1926, he was also involved with the Dartmouth Players, the university drama club. His professors included Marcel Breuer and Walter Gropius.

His first employment, in the fall of 1937, was as a volunteer at the Theater Arts Committee on West 43rd Street in New York City. This was a political haven for theater refugees from Europe, and it attracted a very sophisticated, intellectual crowd. The Committee published a small left-wing magazine called *TAC,* and Herb started by soliciting advertisers as well as doing some editing. He lived in an apartment on West 22nd Street and hung out with artists and actors.

In 1939 Herb joined Fairchild Publications, which published five trade newspapers, including *Women's Wear Daily* and *Menswear Magazine,* and he was sent to Cleveland as national circulation manager. Transferred back to New York in January 1940, he became advertising director of *Menswear,* making $14,000 a year, while spending a small portion of his time on a new publication, *Footwear News.* Although he found the shoe business fascinating, he soon grew frustrated selling advertising and

Portrait of Beth and Herb by Horst.

wanted to make a real product, one that you could hold in your hands, that "served a purpose."[3]

Unable to serve during World War II because he had Perthes disease, which affects the hip joint, Herb stayed in New York. In 1944 he moved down to Perry Street and never lived anywhere but in Greenwich Village for the remainder of his life. In October of that year, Herb joined shoe manufacturer Andrew Geller, the father of his Dartmouth roommate, as sales and advertising manager, taking a pay cut to $12,000 a year. The Geller factory was on Lorimer Street in the Williamsburg section of Brooklyn.[4]

Herbert Levine met Beth Katz when he interviewed her for a design position on June 26, 1946. After a whirlwind courtship, they married four months later on November 3, 1946. Beth reluctantly agreed to join Andrew Geller as his shoe designer for two days a week at $5,000 a year. (Geller said, "What does a girl want with money?"[5]) No one at the company had ever seen a woman in the factory, so they assumed Beth was Geller's daughter. But this newcomer immediately figured out what was wrong with Geller's company: they were perfectly content "copying rather than doing anything original."[6] In a period of less than a year, Beth transformed the company from an "old-ladies' running-boot factory" to a line with a high-fashion look, and it went from fourth in the business to first. She stayed a year and a half, fighting every step of the way to get anything accomplished. (Beth often said that she would have been fired from every job for being "too creative," which is why she and Herb had to start their own business.[7])

Herbert was also frustrated; the company was family-owned and he felt that he would never be promoted to full partner. On December 8, 1948, the day Herb was to ask for a raise, he resigned, not knowing what his next step would be. He had been able to save $7,000 and proposed to take Beth to Europe, planning to deal with their future upon their return to the States.

A couple of weeks after leaving Geller, they went to a Christmas party and were chatting with Sidney Kornblum, the older brother of one of Herb's friends. Beth, with ten years of experience in the footwear industry, and Herb, with four, realized that their individual talents (her creativity and factory knowledge and his

brilliant merchandising methods) complemented each other. A plan was hatched for Kornblum to help them find the $50,000 they needed to form their own company, Herbert Levine, Inc. They postponed the European trip and immediately set about finding a factory and staffing it with experienced shoemakers.

During the war years, 150 million Americans were buying 600 million pairs of shoes annually, all of them made in America.[8] At that time, one needed coupons to buy shoes. The materials for both uppers and soles were being rationed. The retailer had to turn coupons in to the manufacturer to purchase shoes, and the manufacturer had to account to the government for receipt of the coupons. There was a shortage of shoes, so retailers could sell any shoes at any price. Over two hundred shoe factories opened in New York to satisfy the needs of the population, many selling their inventory on the black market.[9] When the war ended, most of the high-end shoe manufacturers went out of business as their costs were too high without the artificial price inflation of the black market. These factories had public auctions and were selling everything to pay their creditors.

The Levines were the only ones looking to start up a shoe factory when everyone else was going out of business. Herb and Beth believed that they could attract consumers by offering original designs manufactured with impeccable quality. They dreamed of designing footwear that had never existed before. They were able to take advantage of the closings of other shoe manufacturers to get what they needed to start their business.

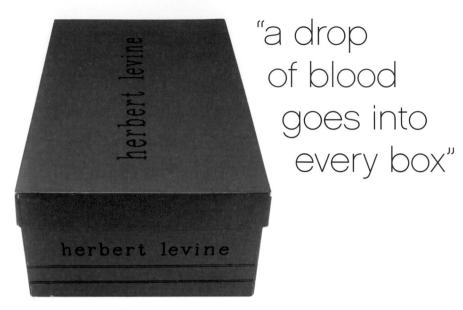

"a drop of blood goes into every box"

The Herbert Levine red shoebox. Font is lowercase American Typewriter.

Their first factory was on the tenth floor of 31 West 31st Street (referred to as "the factory in the sky"), bought in January 1949. They built a 3-by-6-foot sample room, in which only three people could fit at a time. Since two of the people were Herb (the salesman) and Beth (the model), the buyers often had to stand outside in the elevator shaft.

The biannual shoe show was a month away, when buyers from all over would descend on New York to purchase the next season's shoes. The Levines asked an artist, Jeanne Redpath, to make ninety ceramic shoes in her kiln for one dollar each to serve as invitations. They designed a simple primary-red shoebox because "a drop of blood goes into every box."[10] This referred to the blood, sweat, and tears that Herb, Beth, and their workers invested in the two hundred steps it took to fabricate the shoes.

They also needed a name for the shoes. They settled on "Herbert Levine" because "it seemed right that a shoemaker was a man."[11] (When Neiman Marcus gave them their first order for ninety pairs, they were asked to ship them without labels since the buyer wasn't sure how the Jewish-sounding name would be accepted in Texas. By the next season, everyone started to ask for them by name and they became "LEE-vines" in Texas, "La-vins" in Philadelphia, and "Le-VINES" in Chicago.[12])

Most shoe companies at the time employed workers on a per-piece basis, meaning that there would be periods of time when the employees were out of work. Herb always felt it was of paramount importance that their factory stay in operation year-round, and he was the first shoe manufacturer to pay an hourly wage.

The basic steps in making a shoe are cutting, fitting (or stitching), lasting, soling, heeling, finishing, and shipping, each step requiring a space of its own. Shoemaking wasn't as specialized in the postwar years as it has become, and a single factory was expected to produce everything from sandals to closed pumps, in all heel heights, with every toe character, or "shape." The Levines found the best craftsmen, who were, for the most part, immigrants: first-generation Italian lasters; Jewish fitters and stitchers from Poland, Hungary, and Romania; and Irish cutters. They needed an experienced shoemaker to be the factory foreman. They had heard about Louis de Bonis, but were warned not to use him because he was too quality-conscious. At his interview, he told them, "What I know about shoe—it's evil."[13] They hired him on the spot. Tony "Tut" Acuti, who was hired to be their production man, once said, "Here, everyone has to coddle the shoes, handle them, kiss them before they went into a box . . . and then they look up and say 'thank you.'"[14]

Flower Garden, 1951, suede with rhinestone and kidskin flowers at throat and ankle strap, an example of the bestselling *Femme Fatale* series.

The war was over and fashion was rapidly changing. Christian Dior had introduced his "New Look" in 1947. Instinctively sensing the need for lighter and more delicate footwear as an antidote to the heavy platform shoes of the wartime era, Beth designed the first single-soled daytime shoe (referred to as "bead edge," or *ficelle* in French). The Levines' first collection, in February of 1949, consisted of one shoe, named "Femme Fatale," which had a thin wrap-around ankle strap and a V-cut closed-toe vamp on a single sole. They showed it in a myriad of bright colors (which were considered vulgar at the time) and fabrications: satin with colored stones, suede with grosgrain ribbons, kidskin with pearls, and so on. Although Herb had no idea at the time what it actually cost to make a shoe, he priced the "Femme Fatale" at $9.75 wholesale, slightly lower than the market price for similar shoes. The "Femme Fatale" became Herbert Levine's first bestseller, but Herb soon realized that they were losing money and raised his prices. By late 1950, after one year in business and with his shoes selling like hotcakes, Herbert Levine's showroom was visited first by many more buyers than any other vendor. The imitation began and never stopped: Beth's old boss, Max Stollmack of Carlisle Shoe Corporation, copied them "as a sign of friendship" and to show "how much I respect Beth."[15]

In 1949, a majority of the shoe departments in specialty stores were leased. The lessees could decide on their own how they wanted to spend their money and were not yet bound by merchandising managers, so they had more freedom to experiment. One of the Levines' first buyers was Joseph in Chicago, which ordered one thousand pairs to be delivered in May, an astronomical quantity for a factory that had not yet produced a single pair of shoes. By 1951, Joseph in Beverly Hills was doing $495,000 a year in business, with Herbert Levine shoes accounting for $300,000 of it. Other early orders were placed by Famous-Barr in St. Louis, The Blum Store in Philadelphia, Bonwit Teller in Boston, and J. Blach Company in Birmingham.

Jay Jaffee from Harzfeld's in Kansas City gave them the customer letter "Y," because, he said, "*Why* am I buying a new line, like I need a hole in my head?" Jaffee later remarked about buying the Levine line: "No place makes it so difficult. First you have to face Herb, with his questions and interrogations. Then if you pass muster, you have Beth to account to for your shoe knowledge and moral standards."[16]

Beth designed the footwear and Herb handled the factory management, sales, and marketing. Beth was set apart from the other shoe designers of the time because of her experience working on the floor of a factory. One of the biggest obstacles facing a shoe designer is cajoling the patternmaker into trying new ideas. In Beth's case, the patternmaker couldn't get away with telling her that her inventive ideas were impossible, because she knew exactly how they could be made. Because Beth was self-taught, she was freer to question what a shoe could be. Her intention from the beginning was to produce shoes that had never been made before, utilizing the highest-quality workmanship available. Materials, form, and function (i.e., comfort) were always foremost in her mind. She would threaten the factory men with a day of walking in high heels, because she knew that they could only understand comfort if they could imagine wearing the shoes themselves. It was an advantage that Beth wasn't from the traditional background for a designer. She acted more like an artist than a shoe designer, and she broke through gender boundaries in order to rework our very notions of footwear.

Unlike male designers, Beth implicitly understood her customers. She knew every step in making a shoe and followed each prototype throughout the entire production process. She tried on every single shoe that she designed, and was so sensitive to the inside of the shoe that her shoes never cut into the instep and had a reputation for being the best fit in the business. Herb and Beth strove to make shoes that were dramatic and sexy, but above all else practical, agreeing that the consumer is the most important person to please. "Herb listens to me and I listen to anyone who is interested in shoes" was Beth's explanation of why their shoes were consistently ahead of their time.[17]

The Levines had accomplished their dream of making custom shoes in a factory production line; they never compromised quality in order to turn a profit. By 1953, the Levines were doing so well that the fire marshals became concerned about the boxes piled up in the aisles of the factory. For efficiency's sake, the Levines decided to consolidate production on the ninth floor of the Butterick Building at 161 Avenue of the Americas in downtown New York. It became an avant-garde laboratory of invention and quality shoe making, with Beth and Herb overseeing every step of the manufacturing process.

Herbert Levine, Inc. was the first American shoe company to be carried overseas, in the stores of the fashion capitals of Paris (Carel and Galleries Lafayette), London (Harrods), and Stockholm (Nordiska). The Levines were

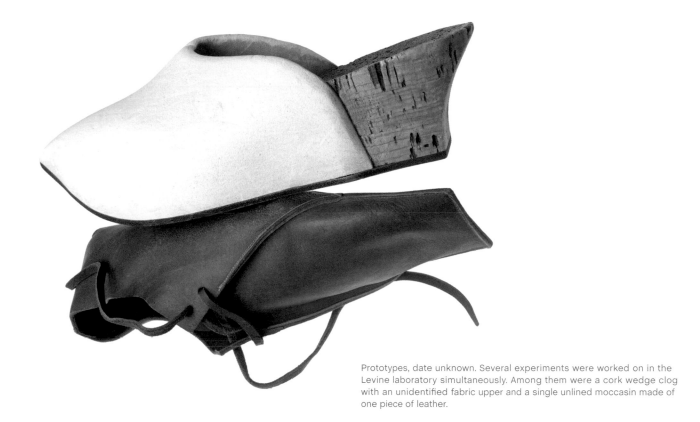

Prototypes, date unknown. Several experiments were worked on in the Levine laboratory simultaneously. Among them were a cork wedge clog with an unidentified fabric upper and a single unlined moccasin made of one piece of leather.

widely known for hand delivering their signature red boxes in an old gray right-hand-drive Rolls Royce, in which they would also chauffeur customers to and from their factory.

But the ever-present challenge was how to continue getting their ingenious concepts to consumers. With Herbert's selling abilities, they knew that if they could only market Beth's innovations directly to women, they would spread like wildfire—as they did, again and again. Starting in 1969, Herbert Levine labels also included Tony the Shoemaker (named after Tony Acuti), Lafitte, Beth's Bootery, and Forann (named for their daughter, Anna). But by the end of the 1960s, the fun started to seep out of their business. Retailers became more cautious, refusing to try new fashion items.

By 1975, the exorbitant price of making shoes in the United States, along with the budding popularity of

sneakers, led Herbert Levine, Inc. to stop production. Herb had had enough; he took care of his employees' pensions and severance, and then he proceeded to shut the doors forever. From the start of their company in 1949 until they closed in 1975, Herbert Levine shoes had become an inspiration to the entire industry. At the time they closed, Herbert Levine, Inc. was making nine hundred pairs of shoes a day (with a gross revenue of $6 million a year) in two factories. The base wholesale price of a plain pump had risen from $9.75 to $24.75 during their twenty-six years of production. Although the Levines had had several offers to license their name, they felt they would lose control of the quality, which was, to them, unthinkable. Herb felt that no licensing arrangement had ever succeeded and pointed to Schiaparelli as an example. "It was just royalties for a name."[18]

inspirations

Beth and Herb Levine believed that "shoes are not only utilitarian but can be works of art."[19] They collected and were inspired by art from the beginning of married life. The abstract expressionist Franz Kline painted their apartment in the mid-1950s (and they later regretted not buying one of his paintings for $800). The contemporary realist painter Philip Pearlstein, whose wife Dorothy was a cousin of Beth, sold his first painting to the Levines. They knew and collected Milton Avery, Chaim Gross, Joseph Solman, and Lilian MacKendrick. Each time they visited the south of France they would buy a Picasso ceramic from the Madoura pottery shop in Vallauris. They also collected Pierre Bonnard, Earl Kirkham, and Paul Signac.

The Levines had their portraits done by Andy Warhol (in a 1960 advertisement for Bonwit Teller), Philip Pearlstein, Joseph Solman (Herb, Beth, and Anna sat for him in his Second Avenue studio), and the fashion photographer Horst.

In addition to art, Beth collected objects from a lifetime of travel. These included a floor-to-ceiling glass case filled with curios such as snuff boxes shaped like shoes, antique lasts, heels, and other shoe-related miniatures. In the étagère were also Dame Alicia Markova's autographed, size 4 1/2B ballet slippers (Dame Markova was the great prima ballerina and director of The Metropolitan Opera Ballet Company) and an antique ivory doll, or *femme de médecin*, which women in the nineteenth century would take to their doctors and use to point out the locations of medical problems. (Beth noted that even these naked ivory figurines had shoes on.)

The Levines used groundbreaking visual art for their advertisements. In the mid-1950s, they incorporated Saul Steinberg's 1954 illustrations from *The Passport* to eye-catching effect. The Levines' spring collection of 1969 was inspired by Jean Dubuffet's signature use of black, white, red, and blue, as in his boxed playing cards, *Banque de l'Hourloupe*, which they had bought in Paris.

During her extensive travels to Europe, Beth also became a pioneering couture collector. In fact, for The Metropolitan Museum's 1973 Balenciaga show, Beth loaned the black chemise which was sketched for the exhibition's poster by Kenneth Paul Block. She was often referred to as one of the chicest women in New York, and her wardrobe included the designs of many of her colleagues, such as Halston, Adele Simpson, Geoffrey Beene, Yves Saint Laurent, and Michael Vollbracht.

Beth Levine was continually influenced by "the street," as well as by popular culture and art. Pop art, moon landings, hippies, and feminism combined to make the 1960s the firm's most creative decade.

Philip Pearlstein, *Beth Levine*, 1985. Oil on canvas, 30 x 24¾ in.

oh,

Herbert,

you

shouldn't

have !

herbert *fine shoes* levine

"Our Beauty". . . one of a collection of Cyrano last pumps for Spring. Oh. . .so many ways!

These whimsical drawings by New York illustrator Saul Steinberg were used in Herbert Levine advertisements, published in the *New Yorker* and *Harper's* in the 1950s. Drawings by Saul Steinberg © The Saul Steinberg Foundation/Artists Rights Society (ARS), New York, originally published in Steinberg, *The Passport*, 1954.

waltz

me

around

again,

Herbert

herbert *fine shoes* levine

Harum-scarum silhouette. Oh... so many ways for spring!

Blue nylon boots with Navajo silver studs and red heel. Photograph by Norman Parkinson, *Vogue*, August 15, 1968.

An example of Herbert Levine's advertisements, which appeared regularly in *Playbill* in the 1950s.

innovations

One of the Levines' merchandising firsts was the notion of naming each of their styles, as well as attaching thumbnail drawings to the shoeboxes so the salespeople didn't have to open them in order to know what was inside. These drawings were done by Beth's sister, Ruthie Ballin, a shoe designer for Saks Fifth Avenue.

The Levines were also the first manufacturers to break away from traditional seasonal marketing by offering four collections a year: resort, spring, fall, and holiday. They recognized that after World War II people were beginning to travel again, and their innovative merchandising plan allowed them to capitalize on this trend. They also defied all preconceptions about appropriate use of materials by using suede for summer, for example, and patent leather for winter.

The company had a revolutionary approach to technology as well as fashion and merchandising. The Levines started out by making four hundred pairs of shoes a week in their factory. In 1951, when the English shoe factories were paying their workers $28 per week, the Levines were paying theirs $120 per week, the highest wages of any shoe workers in the world.[19] By 1954, Herbert Levine, Inc. had two hundred employees making five thousand pairs per week, which made it the sixth-largest shoe-making operation in the country and ten times its original size.

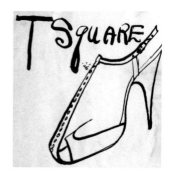

Thumbnail drawings illustrating and naming the shoes were made by Beth's sister, Ruthie Ballin, and were affixed to the outside of the shoebox for easy identification of its contents.

Dorian Leigh, considered the world's first supermodel, wearing the *Gigi Stocking Shoes* by Herbert Levine, black nylon net hosiery permanently attached to high heel satin mules. Photograph by Gjon Mili, *Life*, December 18, 1950, 45.

In early 1950, Beth created the "Gigi Stocking Shoes," which actually resembled lightweight boots. To make these, a stocking was inserted between two layers of sole and drawn up over the foot and leg. Its success was due to the fact that it emphasized a long, unbroken line of leg. It was worn on some of the most famous legs of the time, including those of Marlene Dietrich, who ordered many custom pairs in size 7 1/2B.

In 1951, Herb and Beth finally made their first trip to Europe, which led to their importing the first stiletto, which they called the "String Bean Heel." Although Christian Dior is often credited with introducing the first stiletto, designed by Roger Vivier, in his 1952 show, Beth had actually preceded him. In Paris, Beth and Herb had discovered the thinnest and lightest heels they had ever seen, made by a custom *bottier*, Charles Jordan (*not*

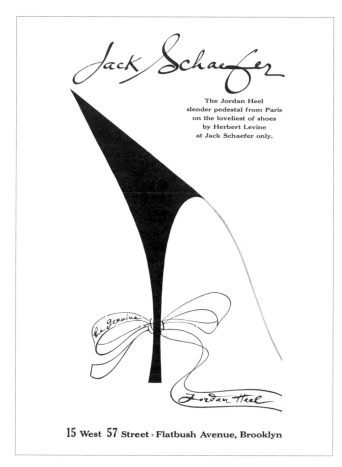

THE STAY-ON SHOE

nstruction makes the barest backless shoe cling to the busiest foot

Above: Advertisement for the *Jordan Heel*, the first stiletto to be sold in the United States. Right: The Herbert Levine "Spring-o-lator" construction, shown in *Life*, May 24, 1954.

Jourdan, Beth repeatedly emphasized). Jordan made shoes to order on the Rue Madeleine and had figured out a way to cut beechwood (instead of turned maple) against the grain, providing more strength than heels had ever had before. Jordan created the first "needle heel" of non-breaking steel at the base and wood at the top. Before the introduction of the "Jordan Heel," later patented by the Levines, nearly 50 percent of wooden heels would break,

so the Levines eagerly arranged a royalty program of five cents a pair with Jordan and brought the new heels to the United States. This sturdy yet glamorous heel became a Levine trademark.

Toward the end of 1952, a man from Boston walked into Herb's office. His name was Maxwell Sachs, and he showed Herb an orthopedic sock lining he had patented as a comfort feature for men's shoes. It was a built-in

bridge of elastic goring that gripped the arch of the foot on a flat moccasin, which he named the "Spring-o-lator." Herb showed the shoe to Beth when she returned to the factory. It was hideously ugly, but a lightbulb went off in Beth's brain. She had always been frustrated with shoe lasts because they were not high enough in the arch for many feet; she wanted the inside of a shoe to caress the arch. She called Louis, her patternmaker, and asked him to tear the vamp (front) and quarter (back) off of a high heel. Then she asked Albert, her stitcher, to devise the lowest-cut vamp imaginable (which they called the "Naked Vamp") and attach the elastic bridge to the insole of the shoe. She then walked in the backless, low-cut mule, and it actually stayed on her foot, even while she was dancing!

The Levines named the first backless shoe "Ballin' the Jack" and showed it to Sachs, agreeing to pay him five cents a pair for the use of the elastic idea, calling it the "Magnet Sock." In 1953, *Glamour* previewed Beth's invention as a "late-day mule with magnetic attraction and the next thing to no shoe at all."[20]

Maxwell Sachs decided not to grant the Levines the six-month exclusive they asked for and showed their high heel to every manufacturer. Everyone copied the "Spring-o-lator" shoe, and some still do.

In 1956, Beth designed the "Cyrano" last, named for its long nose. By means of extra wood added on to a round toe last, the "Cyrano" created some of the most pointed toes the fashion world had seen to date. Trompe l'oeil made the shoe appear smaller than it actually was, creating the illusion that the foot was a size smaller as well.

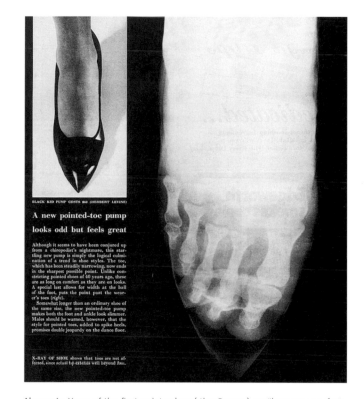

Above: An X-ray of the first pointy shoe (the *Cyrano*), as "long on comfort as it is on looks." The X-ray shows that the toes are not affected by the shape of the shoe, since the actual tip extends well beyond the foot. *Life*, January 21, 1957. **Below:** An example of the *Cyrano* last. **Opposite:** The *No-Shoe.* Image by Milton H. Greene © 2009 Joshua Greene, *Life* magazine, February 17, 1958.

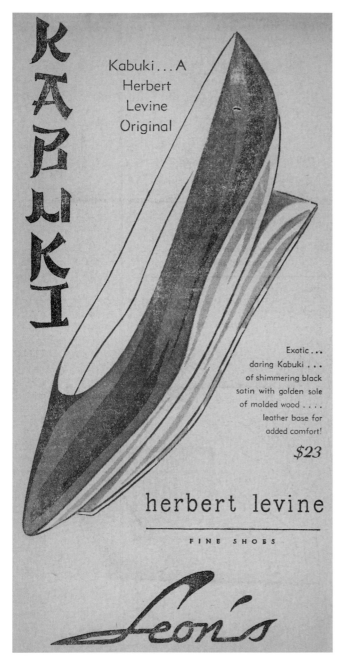

Above: 1963 advertisement for the *Kabuki*. Right: Two versions of *Kabuki*, 1960, in black patent leather (top) and silk with Lurex (bottom).

The following year, the great merchant Stanley Marcus quipped to Beth, "You've done backless and strippy sandals, why not make a shoe without a top?"[21] Never one to turn down a challenge, Beth made the barest shoe possible, the topless "No-Shoe." She had Johnson & Johnson make double-sided surgical pads to keep it on the foot and it was sold with a bottle of adhesive. (This was seven years before Rudi Gernreich designed his topless swimsuit in 1964, showing that once again Beth was ahead of the design curve.)

The aerodynamic "Kabuki" shoes, designed by Beth in 1959, were evocative of shoes worn by traditional Japanese theater performers. This style featured a closed shoe set atop a curved wooden platform, and Beth felt that the shoe looked as if it was floating. She produced many versions of it through the years, including some for Herve Leger's runway show in 1998. Gloria Swanson owned several pairs.

In 1963, Beth contacted Steven Arpad, who did the beading and rhinestone work for Balenciaga in Paris.

Above: *Race Car Shoe*, 1967, kidskin. **Left:** *Mignon*, 1964, hand-glued rhinestones on leather sling pumps, an example of Beth's all-over pavé pumps.

Together they developed a technique for gluing stones to shoes that enabled Beth to create the first fully jeweled shoe, the "Dorothy" pump. When Beth wore a pair of prototypes aboard ship en route to Paris, buyers saw them and they became a sensation before she even reached home. They sold for $200, an exorbitant price at the time, and the retailers couldn't believe that women were actually buying them. In 1967, Liza Minnelli ordered a custom pair of these red pavé pumps for her wedding in homage to her mother, Judy Garland, for whose character in *The Wizard of Oz* the shoe had been named. Beth purchased four thousand red stones and had them glued by hand onto Liza's silk pumps, at a cost of $300.

Beth designed shoes that looked like racing cars for the wife of one of the drivers in the 1967 Indianapolis 500. The driver lost, but Beth had so much fun that she made many more versions over the years, including evening shoes with windshields.

Apollo II landed on the moon on July 20, 1969. What better way to commemorate this historic event than by making moon boots and shoes out of reflective spacesuit material? This was a collaboration with Sara Little Turnbull, who was working with NASA at the time and had been an editor at *House Beautiful*. She and Beth began a noteworthy friendship and became lifetime collaborators. They had the same sample-size foot (4B), were eerily similar in age and family background, and shared a fascination with how products are made. It was to be an enduring and fruitful relationship, and Sara helped to make many of Beth's difficult ideas work.[22]

Beth believed that a great designer should never work in a vacuum, but should always stay in touch with functional considerations. Of utmost importance to her were radical new silhouettes, innovative materials, and whimsical details, but she always kept her common sense.

materials

Herbert Levine shoes were made of a wide variety of materials: cutting-edge synthetics, leather, paper, upholstery fabrics—indeed, anything that could be shaped on a last. One of the Levines' early and enduring goals was to cut leather uppers in one piece, so the shoes would be seamless, which was a very costly proposition. Less expensive lines would cut pieces around the scars and blemishes inherent in leather. Seamless shoes and boots were aesthetically superior but required better-quality (and therefore more expensive) hides.

The Levines were the first Americans in the footwear industry to go to Europe to do business after World War II. While visiting Florence, they bought some elegantly hand-tooled leather boxes as presents for their friends. They located the producer of the boxes, Antinori, in Rome, and made an agreement to send him their uppers so that he could tool the vamps and return them to New York. They also bought a variety of silk ties and decided that the silk from Lake Como was the perfect weight for shoes; they created the first resort collection, the August 1951 "Pearl Diver Collection," out of that fabric.

European producers were willing to grant exclusivity for small runs of fabric, even as little as 35 or 40 yards. Small opening orders from the Levines grew to more than $50,000 orders by the mid-50s. Unlike other shoe manufacturers, the Levines never bought premade designs, but rather found unusual components and interesting materials to experiment with back in their New York City factory. They thought that if they used unique European materials, their shoes couldn't be imitated as easily.

Title unknown, from the *Pearl Diver Collection*, 1951, silk.

Beth began to use transparent vinyl, or Vinylite, in dress shoes; this was considered racy in the early 1950s. In 1952, wishing to create the first truly "invisible" shoe, Herbert asked Beth to devise a method of attaching Lucite heels without the visible screws that manufacturers commonly used. Industrial designer Sara Little Turnbull, Beth's close friend, was working on adhesives at 3M at the time, and she facilitated the first "Cinderella Glass Shoe." Joan Crawford had Vinylite shoes custom made by the Levines because "she loved to see her feet."[23] The popular revival of transparent shoes began in 1964, but it took the cachet of Paris designer Roger Vivier's pumps for Yves Saint Laurent in Spring 1966 for the trend to take hold. Lesley Ann Warren wore Beth's Lucite shoes for the 1965 television version of *Cinderella*.

Beth told a story about the confusion over a French-to-English translation of the original *Cinderella*,

Japanese workers making Levine heels, 1955.

written by Charles Perrault in 1697. It seems that the words *pantoufle de verre* (slipper of glass) were originally *pantoufle de vair* (slipper of fur). The famed glass slipper in later versions of the Cinderella tale was a result of this mistranslation.

In the early 1950s the Levines used brocades, silk, and novelty leather from around the globe; it was not until 1954 that printed leathers were being produced in American tanneries. The Levines would find the source of a Picasso-print *peau-de-soie* handbag in France and use the fabric to make a few pairs of sample shoes. They would buy silk from Italy and Spain, velvets from Lyons, cotton and linen from England, and send the fabrics back to their New York City factory to experiment with.

Beth and Herb were also known for their incredible ornamentation. For example, Beth loved the nail heads on Line Vautrin's jewelry, found in a shop across from the

Bristol Hotel, where they stayed in Paris. They contracted the manufacturer, Madame Goepfer, whose studio was on the outskirts of Paris, and as a result, Herbert Levine shoes had the finest cut-steel nail heads in the world.

Following the Levines' trip to China, Japan, Thailand, Burma, India, and Egypt in early 1955, their shoes took on some distinctly Far Eastern accents. They began to import heels from Kurihara in Japan. They found a family in the mountains who was working with inlaid mother of pearl and sampled some heels. Beth even devised a way to make heels out of woven bamboo. They would send their French or Italian silk to Japan, have it hand embroidered by the firm employed by the emperor of Japan, and have it sent back to New York.

It was always difficult to get the American leather tanneries to invest in researching new products, so the Levines spent a lot of time in Europe. Here is a classic story told by Beth, describing why it was more rewarding to work with European suppliers.

We bought some beautiful suede— it was "non-crock," meaning the colors didn't crack or rub off. Hermes used it for clothes and bags. I wanted to meet the tanner so we arranged a meeting in a small town ten miles from Limoges. I had seen a fantastic rose on the Riviera—it was the most velvety rose I had ever seen. The name of the rose was Baccarat. Could Santro [the tanner] duplicate that incredible color?

Ordinarily, if you were going to place an order you'd have to purchase 2,000 feet, broken up by skins. We got the leather and it was perfect; beautiful but not the exact color I was looking for. It was red but it wasn't the color of the Baccarat rose. I had been looking for a particular kind of leather to make a new boot, and while we were going through the factory I saw something that would be perfect. I told Herb that we needed to get a leather with a smooth finish and here it was—the smoothest, most beautiful leather, that worked on both sides.

We went into the area where he did the coloring, a small room with high ceilings and windows so dirty you couldn't see through them. There was one bare light hanging from the ceiling. No one could believe what he did with colors. It turns out that he indeed had a peculiar thing with his eyes. He could see like a cat in the dark and had a mind-boggling capability to see color.

Before we went to visit him, I tried to find a Baccarat rose to bring. My agent in Paris sent him one but it was dead when he received it. We inspired him to do things with leather never done before. The pleasure is finding a guy like Santro.[24]

They bought leather from Santro instead of from American tanneries from that day on.

Herb would work with our suppliers and give them orders when they needed them. For instance, we bought reptile from a tannery in Switzerland. They worked with exotics like snakeskin, lizard, and python. The widow ran the business and needed business year-round. Herb would supply her with orders during their "down time" and, in turn, she would bend over backwards for us. There was a certain color bronze I was looking for at the time—no one had it. I remember seeing a kidskin somewhere else with the color, but it turned purple. I asked the woman to try to make it without turning it purple. She did it by putting a thin plastic film on it—and the process worked on silver and gold as well. Yves Saint Laurent went crazy when he saw the bronze leather [at the Semaine de Cuir]. The woman got the idea from us and was amazed that I had created something that French designers wanted. We gave the tannery more business than YSL, but our work together was being sold to many top fashion designers. This is how we were able to get what we wanted from suppliers.[25]

The mid-1960s marked the beginning of disposable culture: throwaway cigarette lighters, paper diapers, and paper clothes. Beth felt compelled to make paper shoes to match, and an opportunity soon presented itself. Kathryn Stoll Paige, a graphic designer, approached the Levines at the behest of Gloria Moncur, editor of *Harper's Bazaar*. Paige had made some paper shoes that she was interested in having the Levines produce. The shoes were composed of brightly colored, double-faced, laminated paper strips twisted into exquisite swirls and multicolor bands that flexed on composition soles. Beth called them "just right for your at-home costumes."[26] Her keen sense of irony also inspired her to make mules from paper money and day-old newspapers.

Beth experimented with every kind of jeweled and decorated heel. She glued rhinestones to the insides of heels. She forged heels out of the same aluminum used to

Assorted paper shoes, 1967.

Title unknown, 1961, lizard Mary Jane on teakwood sculpted heel. Before Beth began using teak in heels for shoes, clogs, and sandals, it was being used in the 1950s for Danish Modern furniture and home decor.

Barefoot in the Grass, 1966, AstroTurf insole, vinyl vamp, green kid heel. Beth's *Barefoot in the Grass* series demonstrates her witty use of contemporary and unexpected materials.

make airplane wings for the air force. She fashioned heels and wedges out of teakwood (commonly used for salad bowls), as well as beech and mahogany, which, until that time, were used primarily to build furniture.

Beth launched the pilgrim buckle with her "Tom Jones Collection" in the fall of 1964. Although Roger Vivier is often credited with this style, he actually designed his first large gold buckle for Yves Saint Laurent's collection in the summer of 1965, almost a full year after Beth had premiered it.

The Levines continued to demonstrate that shoes could be made of almost anything, such as beaver tail, frog skin, sheep's belly, and horsehair. Notable designs included leather heels folded in on themselves, strips of paper or vinyl twisted to resemble ribbon candy, and AstroTurf insoles—all incorporated into the Levine line, with varying degrees of success.

In 1972, the Levines' hottest shoe was a simple wedge pump with crepe soling, the "Chinese Slipper." "I thought it would be nice if we could have the comfort in our leather dress shoes that could be enjoyed in sneakers. We put crepe soles on patent leather and kid and calf—a wedge pump and moccasin first, then a sandal and a boot. We had to cut plantation crepe, experimented, and made mixtures ourselves for adhesives to keep the soles on and not peel like a banana."[27] When the Levines first brought out the shoe, only three stores bought it. By the next year, when both Halston and Geoffrey Beene featured it with their collections, Bonwit Teller alone sold 3,500 pairs. By 1972, the factory was making 1,100 pairs per day of that one construction.

boots

Fashion historians credit Beth with being the first person to incorporate boots into haute couture. The Levines were the only ones producing dress boots in the early 1960s; their boots were never copied because no one else considered boots a fashion element. Manufacturers at the time regarded boots as a totally different classification from shoes, used only for inclement weather or work. Beth, on the other hand, never considered boots as a separate entity, but rather as an extension of an outfit. Popular demand backed up her theory that "a boot IS a shoe."

In 1953, Beth introduced a mid-calf white kidskin boot. (This was eleven years before French designer André Courrèges made his "go-go boots.") Retailers initially laughed at her mid-calf boot and didn't buy. Eugenia Sheppard wrote, "Everyone thought it was a big joke and were still laughing in 1959 when she made a whole collection of them."[28]

Miniskirts paved the way for Beth's next boot innovation: the first seamless, stretch-vinyl pull-on boot. Beth had found an upholstery fabric made in Italy that consisted of urethane blended with nylon (to smooth more easily over furniture). She convinced the manufacturer of the fabric to adapt the product for boots, and soon the entire world was seeking it out. The challenge was how to get the last out of the stretch boot. Once Beth solved that dilemma, she introduced the "Female Boot," the first zipperless knee-high boot. She billed it as a boot for "the liberated leg," one that flattered all shapes and sizes.[29]

Elizabeth Semmelhack, curator of The Bata Shoe Museum, noted, "They [the vinyl boots] were never

Treat me kindly

I am a fashion shoe . . . called a BOOT.

I was created to be soft, light, elegant and divinely comfortable.

I was not intended to be a snow boot or a rubber boot. I have Kid Leather insides.

I am water-repellent . . . not waterproof or scuff-proof.

I am the finest boot made, and a delightful experience to wear. But, I cannot be guaranteed beyond normal shoe wear.

Insert in boot box explaining that these are fashion boots, not utilitarian.

fetishistic, yet always had an edge."[30] In an example of retailers playing it safe, there had been one pair of stretch-vinyl boots out on the sales floor of Saks Fifth Avenue by mistake, the intention having been to return them to the factory. A customer tried the boots on and refused to take

Enclosing all the body in yards of silk chiffon, The Scarf Shoe—flying upwards from a jeweled heel. Each Scarf Shoe, a free-flowing stocking based on a solid sole, covers the leg and leaves long streamers to twine around the body. By Herbert Levine, in Gourdin hand-painted silk chiffon. About $250. At Bonwit Teller.
—*HARPER'S BAZAAR*, APRIL 1968

them off. She wore the boots out of the store and they created a fashion frenzy. "They thought we were crazy," Beth said, "but, you know what? They sold!"[31]

Beth designed boots that were also pants, "over-the-shoulder" boots, thigh-high boots attached with garter belts, waist-high stocking boots attached to girdles, one-piece boot dresses, and even a whimsical "Scarf Shoe."

Beth's constant complaint was that retailers did not accept her most innovative designs, and her stretch-vinyl line was no exception. These form-fitting boots had simply never existed before; nervous store buyers didn't know what to make of these sexy, cutting-edge boots. They could be worn with everything from minis and maxis to pants and shorts.

Carels in Paris began to carry Beth's boots in 1966, and soon chic women throughout Europe were wearing them as well. Vivian Infantino, the legendary fashion editor of *Footwear News*, wrote:

> The first truly tight-fitting knee-highs were Beth's 1965 versions, glossy seamless stretch boots that set the tone for a new boot category and launched the use of synthetics in high fashion lines. The boots were made of a patent-look polyurethane that enabled Beth to create the hug-the-foot look that was radically different from anything on the fashion scene.[32]

Beth's boots became so popular that when Nancy Sinatra needed boots for her 1966 hit "These Boots Are Made for Walkin'," she naturally went to Beth for the white go-go boots that became a cultural icon. The Levines opened Beth's Bootery on the fourth floor of Saks Fifth Avenue in New York on February 16, 1970. It was the

Above: Nancy Sinatra wearing Beth's boots on television.
Opposite: The *Scarf Shoe*. Photograph by Guy Bourdin, *Harper's Bazaar*, April 1968.

Left to right: *Vasarely Sandal*, 1971, velour suede with gold dot accenting suede diamond. *Two To One*, 1971, black velvet; a stretch-up-the-leg look that stays put, used in Halston's collection. *Dress Parade*, 1971, nylon and stretch crepe.

first time a retailer featured an American shoe designer by name. Beth was given carte blanche to sell new colors and avant-garde styles, which were replenished weekly. It became a design laboratory, and Beth's Booteries were soon opened at Saks in Washington, D.C., Detroit, Chicago, and Beverly Hills. In the spring of 1971 she created "Legcitement," which included knee-high gladiator sandal-boots. The Levines' factory superintendent remarked that in his forty-five years of working in shoe factories, he had never seen so many varieties of shoes and boots in one season.

celebrity clients

Both Herb and Beth adored the theater and were deeply involved in new productions on Broadway, both as investors and by shoeing the actresses. They felt that actors were their most exacting customers. "We made a pair of shoes for Bette Davis," Beth recounted. "I told her that I could make a soft sole for the stage, which looked like leather but was soft, didn't make noise, and didn't slip. She loudly exclaimed, 'I hate pussyfooting . . . I WANT TO BE HEARD!'"[33] Marilyn Monroe purchased red stilettos (size 7AA) by the Levines from Vogue Shoe Shop in Montreal in 1957; they are now in the collection of The Bata Shoe Museum in Toronto.

Herbert Levine shoes were worn by fashionable women of all ages. The shoes were so comfortable that they became favorites of First Ladies, whose duties included standing and walking for long periods of time. Beth is often referred to as "the First Lady of shoes" because of this. The Levines made black velvet knee-high boots for Mamie Eisenhower as well as most of her pumps. Beth designed shoes for Lady Bird Johnson and her daughters, Lynda Bird and Lucy Baines, for Lyndon B. Johnson's 1965 inauguration; Lady Bird's were yellow satin evening shoes.

Beth also designed shoes for Patricia Nixon and her daughters, Tricia and Julie, for both the 1969 and the 1973 inaugural balls.[34] Beth was once summoned to the White House to coordinate all of Mrs. Nixon's shoes with her wardrobe. At first, Mrs. Nixon was very conservative and thought of boots as unfeminine. Beth prevailed, and the First Lady bought her first pair of black knee-high boots.

Over time, Beth delivered over thirty pairs of shoes and boots to the Nixon women. She was also enlisted to do the footwear for Tricia's 1971 White House wedding to Edward Cox, whose mother, Mrs. Howard Ellis Cox, was also a fan of Levine shoes.

Beth had to juggle her showroom appointments so that Patricia Nixon wouldn't have to run into Jacqueline Kennedy, another First Lady who wore the Levine label. For Mrs. Kennedy, Beth custom-made a pair of thigh-high boots in burlap with a stacked heel, as well as many of the flats that became a signature element of the iconic Jackie Kennedy style.

Barbra Streisand, a shy nineteen-year-old, came to the design studio on Sixth Avenue when she was first cast in the original production of *Funny Girl* on Broadway in 1964. She desperately wanted a pair of antique lace-up brown leather boots, and Beth dragged her to a full-length mirror and whispered in the Brooklynite's ear in Yiddish, "Don't make yourself ugly."

Dinah Shore had extremely mismatched feet and had her shoes custom-made at the Levine factory. Sizing is always difficult, Beth said, because "after all, two feet just don't match."[35]

Another story involved Janis Paige in the stage version of *Miracle on 34th Street* in 1963. She was to play a chic, stern fashion editor. "I thought she would wear a flat heel, which was just entering the fashion picture," Beth recounted. "But she was the actress and explained to me that the heel was the tip-off to her true character. I designed a pair of black crocodile high-heel stilettos,

Did it ever occur to you that the real explanation for Pat Nixon's blissful smile on Inauguration Day could have been that her feet weren't killing her?

—BETTY OMMERMAN, *NEWSDAY*, JANUARY 24, 1969

Top: Inaugural shoes for Patricia Nixon, 1973, turquoise silk-crepe T-strap halter back. **Above:** Marilyn Monroe's red stilettos, 1957.

because, she said, 'underneath the executive veneer was really a feminine girl who couldn't give up her high heels.'"[36]

Beth designed for three *Mame*s, most notably Angela Lansbury in 1966. Thanks to Beth's ingenuity in creating a special heel—attractive yet functional, with a strategically set piece of thin rubber that ensured her safety—Miss Lansbury succeeded in flying up and down stairs with grace, and without falling. Shirley MacLaine wore Beth's designs in the plays *Sweet Charity* (1966) and *Irma la Douce* (1961), as did Eydie Gorme in the Broadway show *Golden Rainbow* (1968). The Levines were asked in 1964 to invest in the original Broadway production of *Fiddler on the Roof*, a musical set in a shtetl that tells the story of a Jewish dairy farmer with five daughters. Beth declined, explaining her reluctance with the comment, "Who would be interested in my life?"[37]

In addition to their popularity with presidents' wives and actors on Broadway, Herbert Levine shoes were also a nonstop favorite of movie stars and socialites. Clients included Jane Fonda, Joanne Woodward, Lauren Bacall, Barbara Walters, Julie Andrews, Rita Hayworth (stretch loop sandal), Raquel Welch, Mrs. Cornelius Vanderbilt Whitney (for Charles James), Peggy Lee, Cyd Charisse, Joan Collins, Cher, Linda Evans, Babe Paley (who didn't know her own shoe size, as all her shoes had previously been custom-made in Paris), Rosemary Clooney, Betty Grable, Gladys Knight, Natalie Wood, Debbie Reynolds, Arlene Francis, Phyllis Diller (who ordered six pairs of ankle boots), Helen Hayes, Chita Rivera, Joan Sutherland, Gwen Verdon, Liv Ullman, Agnes de Mille, Carol Channing, Ali MacGraw, and Barbara Hale, who made "Spring-o-lators" a trademark of her character Della Street on the television show *Perry Mason*.

The Levines continued their love affair with the theater throughout their careers; they designed shoes for Elaine Stritch and all the women in *Company* (1970). Herbert Levines were a favorite of film costume designers as well, appearing in *The Great Gatsby* (1974), with costumes designed by Theoni Aldrich.

Cher, boots by Beth Levine, New York, August 20, 1969. Photograph by Richard Avedon. © 2009 The Richard Avedon Foundation.

awards, honors, press, and collaborations

From the earliest days of Herbert Levine, Inc., the fashion press reported on the new company. June Cuniff and later Gloria Moncur at *Harper's Bazaar*, Sally Kirkland at *Life*, Joann Zill at *Look*, and Geraldine Stutz (the legendary president of Henri Bendel) at *Glamour* were all avid supporters of the innovations emerging from the Levine factory on an almost weekly basis. In 1954, the Levines won the first of their many awards, the coveted Neiman Marcus Award for excellence in fashion.

Throughout her career, Beth collaborated with the fashion arbiters of the time. She fashioned a shoe out of peacock plumes (now in The Metropolitan Museum's Costume Institute) for Gene Moore for the store windows at Tiffany's in 1958. Mr. Moore and Beth did another shoe-themed window together in 1966.

Beginning in 1966, Beth worked with Emilio Pucci to create groundbreaking uniforms for the stewardesses at Braniff International Airlines. These landmark uniforms included clear plastic boots and graphic two-color shoes. Alexander Girard designed the graphics and the fabric, Pucci the clothes, and Levine the footwear.

Throughout the life of Herbert Levine, Inc., Herb and Beth collaborated with many great fashion designers for their runway shows, including Halston (Beth introduced ultrasuede to him, having failed to make it work for shoes), Pauline Trigère, Oleg Cassini, Victor Costa, George Halley, Adolfo, Geoffrey Beene, Bill Blass, Adele Simpson, Charles James, and Oscar de la Renta. Eleanor Lambert, an iconic fashion journalist from the *New York Herald Tribune*, wrote all of the Herbert Levine press releases.

Braniff International, 1966. Emilio Pucci designed the dresses, hats, raincoats, and plastic helmets for Braniff hostesses, and Beth designed the boots.

Beth appeared on *What's My Line?* wearing an outfit by George Halley, who was working for Charles James. She also appeared with Joyce Brothers on *Today* on August 16, 1973.

The fashion press honored Beth Levine with her first Coty American Fashion Critics' Award in 1967. William Claxton and Peggy Moffit made a short film of Herbert Levine shoes for the presentation. Beth received a second Coty award in 1972. She was the only shoe designer ever to win twice.

Top left: Neiman Marcus Award winners for 1954, Beth and Herbert Levine, accept their silver and ebony plaque from store president Stanley Marcus at the famous Texas specialty store's Fashion Exposition opening night, September 6, 1954. **Top right:** From Emilio Pucci's 1965 Gemini IV collection, *The Airstrip*, for Braniff Airlines. Levine designed the two-tone calfskin boots and shoes. **Above:** Herbert and Beth Levine being presented with the Coty American Fashion Critics' Award, 1967. From left: C. Z. Guest, unknown, Herbert and Beth Levine, Pat Peterson.

later years

Beth loved a challenge, and she never abandoned an idea because of its inherent difficulty. In a speech delivered to the Department of Commerce in 1978 she said, "Manufacturers will just have to adjust their thinking to modern times and be able to turn on a dime like a good polo pony. If open shoes are desirable, make them good and stop complaining. Establish a factory attitude that flexes with the times. It is just as easy and takes the same time to do something well, as half well."[38]

The Levines lived in a terrace apartment on West 12th Street for fifty years. Their daughter, Anna, and her twin boys, William Davidson Thomson III and H. Hugo Thomson, lived on half of the full floor, with Herb and Beth, and then Beth alone, occupying the other side. The large roof terrace was planted with trees, flowers, vegetables, and herbs that Beth used for cooking. Beth adored entertaining and was a fantastic cook, often equating cooking with designing.

Enjoying the inspiration of nature, Herb and Beth would spend weekends at their summer home in Westhampton Beach, Long Island, not far from the farm where Beth grew up. Her nephew, Ron Bush, and his family still own a part of the family farm, where they grow vegetables, stable horses, and have turned a barn into a museum of farm implements, with a special section devoted to Beth's shoes.

Herbert was Beth's biggest supporter, agreeing with her that the only mistake is "playing it safe." He always pushed Beth to realize her dreams, and to entertain him in the process. Together they were able to introduce revolutionary silhouettes in improbable fabrics that fit perfectly. Often called the finest salesman and merchandising manager in the world, Herb was revered by his employees and business associates. He once noted, "for twenty-seven years, I counted pairs, not sheep to go to sleep at night."[40] "We had fun because he wouldn't fire me if I did something nutty," she said.[40] Their innovations have earned unparalleled admiration that has stood the test of time.

Herbert Levine died of lung cancer at their Westhampton home in 1991. In 1999, The Bata Shoe Museum in Toronto, Canada, exhibited a retrospective of the Levines' work, entitled "Herbert and Beth Levine: An American Pair." This retrospective was the culmination of Beth's fifty-year professional relationship and close friendship with Sonja Bata, who was, and remains, an early and fervent admirer of Beth's brilliance. Elizabeth Semmelhack from The Bata Shoe Museum says about Beth's designs:

> American ingenuity pervaded her designs without the burden of class. Because of her wry sense of wit, Beth was able to use non-shoe materials that carried other meanings (i.e., AstroTurf, newspaper) and not simply "decorate" a shoe. Her wit was not superficial, but, rather, came from the structure of the shoe outward, or tearing through the skin of a shoe.[41]

Up until her death in 2006, Beth was still working and consulting with design luminaries such as Azzedine Alaïa, Helmut Lang, and Herve Leger. She lectured and spoke at various universities and industry events. Beth Levine died of lung cancer at her 12th Street apartment on September 20, 2006, still full of energy, wisdom, and bold ideas.

Portrait of Beth Levine by Bruce Weber, 1999.

Beth spoke Yiddish as elegantly as she spoke French. She could sip her scotch and tell risqué jokes to royalty and truck drivers alike—in other words, "she was the life of the party." Her shoe designs were world famous, but what she loved most was that she was always a farm girl who knew a good tomato when she saw one. —BRUCE WEBER

HER WORK

If a shoe is beautiful and it doesn't fit the foot, it's not a quality shoe. It must fit the foot and the eye.

BETH LEVINE, *FOOTWEAR NEWS*, APRIL 8, 1974

Perfect Pump, 1952
Black satin pump, squared vamp with stuffed velvet at throat, pink satin lining.

The architecture of these shoes speaks to Beth's constant striving for perfection in shape.

Concerto, 1952
Red suede halter with rhinestone and jet ornament; rhinestones on breasting of black patent heel.

Beth was always searching for hidden and unusual ways to embellish shoes, taking particular interest in the underside or inside heel.

A shoe is like a brassiere worn on the outside—there's a certain amount of sex attached to them.

JOSEPH MAGNIN ADVERTISEMENT, 1962

Men are convinced that a woman's legs are glorified by high heels, especially the instep, which takes on the curve of the bosom.

BETH LEVINE, *BOSTON EVENING GLOBE*, APRIL 4, 1972

Ballin' the Jack, 1953
Two versions of "Spring-o-lator" or "Magnet" mules. Top pair is woven silk, bottom pair is silk with Lurex print.

First appearing in *Glamour* in April 1953, Beth's backless mules were referred to as having "magnetic attraction" and being "the next best thing to no shoe at all." Today, vintage "Spring-o-lators" are highly collectible, and designers including Moschino and Stella McCartney use them in their sandals.

I design
shoes not
because you need
them but because
you want them.

BETH LEVINE

Bubbling Over, circa 1953
Printed raw silk with applied rhinestones, wrap-around ankle strap.

The Levines constantly scoured the world for new and exciting materials. These were made of French silk, and rhinestones were applied by hand in the New York factory.

It was the sensation of the time. I was running to meet my husband in a café in Cannes, and two Englishmen followed me to see how my shoes stayed on!

BETH LEVINE, *ELLE*, 1992

Ballin' the Jack, 1953
Silk gingham high-heel mule.

Always striving to make the most sensual shoes possible, Beth designed the first high-heel backless sandals, which hugged the arch by means of an elastic bridge, commonly referred to as a "Spring-o-lator."

To Beth and Herbert Levine, who step into the fashion foreground with shoe designs of such architectural and sculptural perfection that they might have come from Da Vinci's notebooks.

STANLEY MARCUS, 1954

Prototype with pearl ornament, circa 1954
Unlined satin stiletto with breasted heel, leather sole,
and pearl beads on wire.

Thanks to Beth's wild creativity, the Herbert Levine factory made thousands of prototypes, experimenting with every conceivable type of toe, heel shape, material, and ornamentation.

I don't know who invented the high heel, but all women owe him a lot.

MARILYN MONROE

Left: Title unknown, 1954. Gold lamé stiletto
Right: Title unknown, 1955. Black and gold Lurex stiletto

One of the most high-profile fans of the Levines' sensuous high heels was Marilyn Monroe. Both in her private life and in Richard Avedon's iconic photographs of her, Monroe showcased the glamour of the Herbert Levine label.

Title unknown, 1955
French silk, hand-embroidered vamp and heel
cover, halter with rhinestone buckle.

The first American shoe manufacturers to do business in the Far East after World War II, the Levines
found embroiderers who worked for the emperor
of Japan. The Levines often sent fabric from France
and Italy to Japan for handwork, to be assembled
later in their factory in New York.

Building a shoe is
like building a house.
There must be a
good foundation, it
must be right before
you embellish it with
landscaping and color.

BETH LEVINE, *MCCALL'S*, NOVEMBER 1968

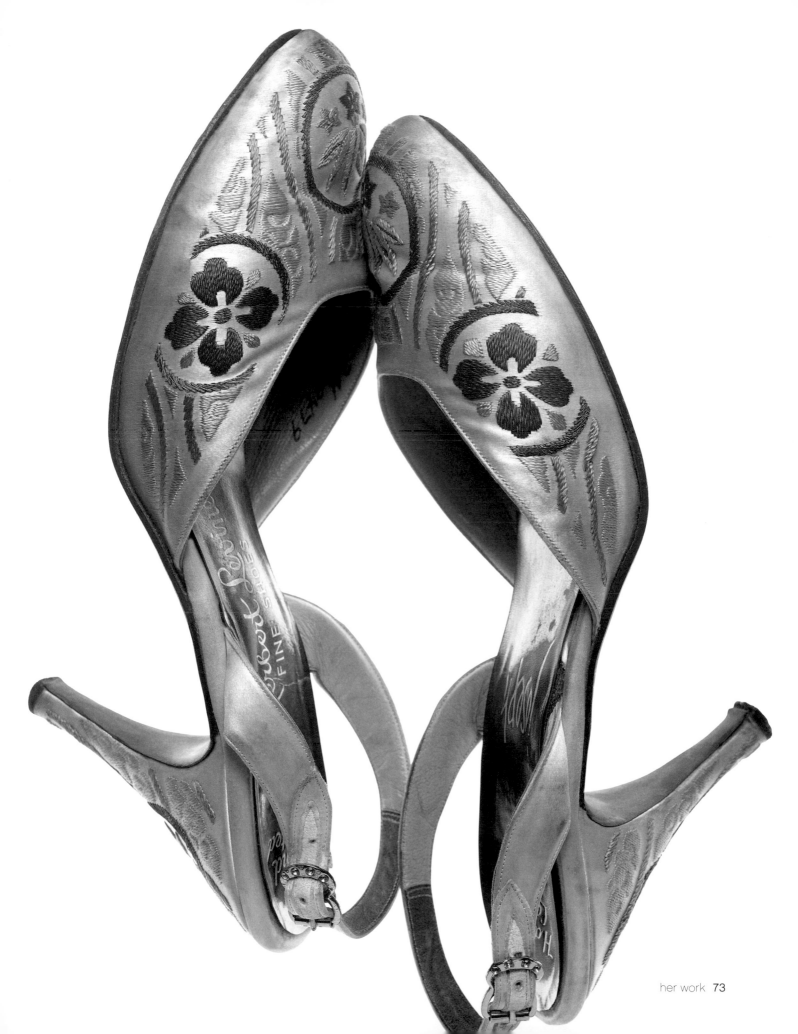

Under Construction, 1955
**Black leather open-toed slingback
with gold studs under arch.**

Under Construction was revolutionary
in that it has only a half-sole under the
ball of the foot, and the underside of the
arch is embellished leather so the shoe
will "fit like a glove."

The only designs that count are the originals. Nothing is really important if someone else has done it before.

HERBERT LEVINE,
RETROSPECTIVE AT THE COSTUME
INSTITUTE AT THE METROPOLITAN
MUSEUM OF ART, 1976

Free Form, 1956
**Tan leather mule with white topstitching,
wide, buckled vamp and instep straps,
geometric sole with sharp pointed toe, and
sculpted heel.**

Beth was awarded countless design patents
for her inventions, including one for the shape
of this sole.

Fashion is synonymous with change; glamour is the unifying theme.

BETH LEVINE TO MARIAN CHRISTY, *OAKLAND TRIBUNE,*
FEBRUARY 19, 1975

T-Flap, 1956
**Pink satin, rhinestone nail heads, leather lining
and sole, buckle.**

This paradoxical design has an open toe that is
partially covered. The T-strap is a continuation of
the sole and can be worn under or over the vamp.
It sold for $29.95 in 1956.

The shape of a shoe is more important than the shape of a dress.

BETH LEVINE, *CHARLESTON DAILY MAIL*, FEBRUARY 20, 1971

Title unknown, 1956
Silk jacquard pump with snipped
toe, black satin lining.

The ultimate perfectionist, Beth used the most exquisite fabrics on deceptively simple shapes.

To find beauty
in form instead
of finding it in
ornament is
the goal toward
which humanity
is aspiring.

ADOLPH LOOS

Tuxedo, 1956
Tricolor silk satin pump with bow.

When Beth began designing, bold colors in footwear were considered vulgar. She constantly mixed colors conventionally deemed clashing or in bad taste, often with spectacular results.

They'll probably spray them on!

BETH LEVINE, ON BEING ASKED ABOUT THE SHOE OF THE FUTURE,
WOMEN'S WEAR DAILY, JULY 24, 1963

No-Shoe, 1957
Silk, leather, adhesive pads.

These topless shoes were designed on a dare from Stanley Marcus, founder of Neiman Marcus, seven years before Rudi Gernreich's iconic topless swimsuits. The shoes came with a bottle of adhesive; the wearer would brush the liquid on the ball-of-foot and heel surgical pads manufactured by Johnson & Johnson. This bottle, in the collection of the Dutch Shoe Museum, is the only known surviving example.

She has a
notion of a shoe that
creates energy through
the simple act of walking.
She concedes, "I'm going
to dream."

THE TORONTO STAR, JUNE 10, 1999

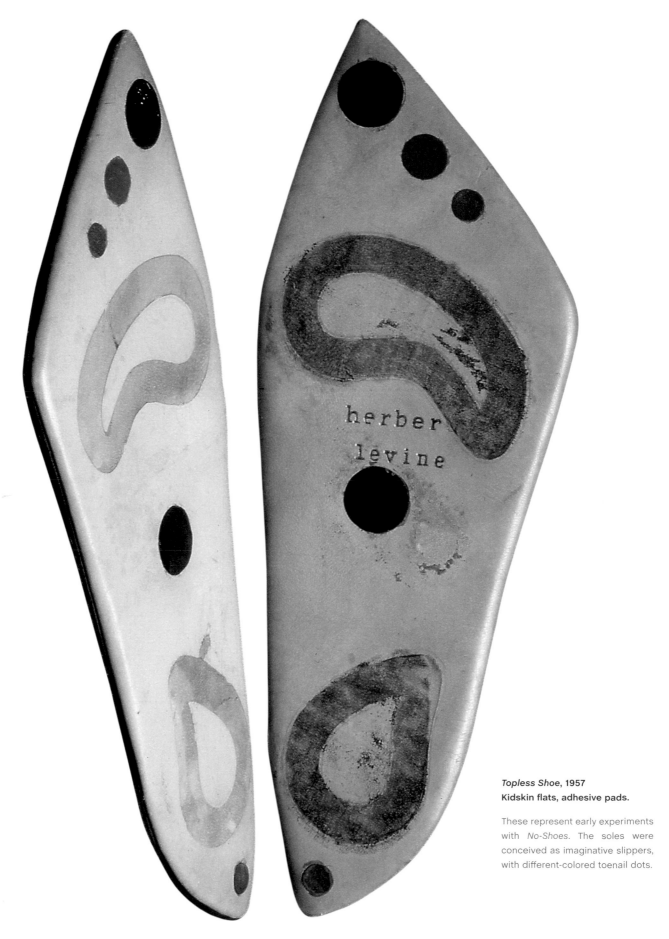

Topless Shoe, 1957
Kidskin flats, adhesive pads.

These represent early experiments with *No-Shoes*. The soles were conceived as imaginative slippers, with different-colored toenail dots.

Luckily, when I got the idea of doing a shoe in peacock feathers, I knew just the person to turn to. So I took the peacock feathers to Beth Levine and selected the shoe I wanted, and she made a pair. She loved the idea so much that she kept the other one!

GENE MOORE, *WINDOWS AT TIFFANY'S: THE ART OF GENE MOORE*, 1980

Peacock Shoe, 1958
Leather, silk satin, and peacock feathers.

This iconic shoe appeared in the window of Tiffany in 1958 with Jean Schlumberger's jewels. Gene Moore collaborated with Beth on another window in 1966.

Sea Mist, 1958
Black silk satin pump with hand-applied, varie-gated, multicolored rhinestones on vamp.

Beth was a couture collector, and her favorite European designer was Balenciaga. Beth worked with the artisan who did all of Balenciaga's bead and rhinestone work. These shoes are an example of the handmade quality of Herbert Levine shoes.

Dressing is like cooking—you taste. I learned by doing.

BETH LEVINE TO HELENE VERIN

Diana Vreeland wanted a shoe with a low heel, turned up at the toe, open yet closed, and with jewels on it. I designed a shoe with a big circle at the toe, inside of which I hung a rhinestone ball.

BETH LEVINE, *DIANA VREELAND: IMMODERATE STYLE*

Aladdin's Lamp, 1959
Gold kidskin mule with rhinestone ornament, gold wood platform with low spool heel.

Inspired by the 1954 film *The Barefoot Contessa*, starring Ava Gardner, this shoe was designed at the request of the inimitable Diana Vreeland, fashion editor of *Harper's Bazaar*.

Happiness is
a pair of Herbert
Levine shoes!

AUDREY SMALTZ, *EBONY*, 1973

Title unknown, 1959
Printed geometric-patterned silk mule with cotton striped insole and covered heel.

The mule was an essential part of Beth's oeuvre. She often placed a padded velvet heart on the insole. It was raised, thereby "hugging the arch" to help the foot stay put.

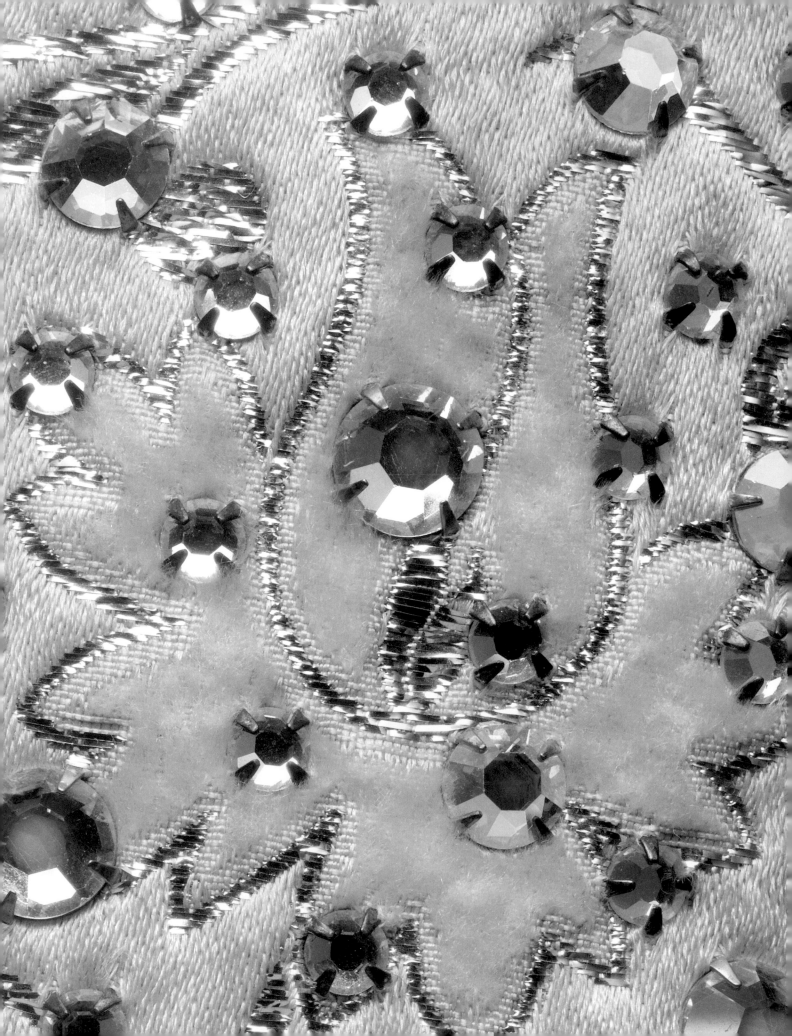

Theatre Boot, 1959
**Ivory silk boot with gold embroidery,
studded with two sizes of clear and
iridescent stones.**

Beth frequently used the French saying
"venez y voir," which means "come and
see." Specifically, it refers to fashion that
uses embroidery and trim or is decorated
with jewels. Reminiscent of eighteenth-
century styles, this fashion rewards those
who come for a closer look. These boots
are a luxurious example.

***Anemone d'Orsay*, 1959**
Pink suede d'Orsay with lavender plastic flower ornament.

While looking through a dusty box of buckles and bows from the Levine factory, I came upon an ugly plastic flower and couldn't imagine how Beth could have made anything chic with it. Then I found these shoes! Beth loved to mix high and low, or cheap and expensive.

Ideas are easy to come by. Getting them realized is something else.

BETH LEVINE, ORAL HISTORY, 1972

Ideas I snatch from the air—ideas that aren't there yet. But that's the exhilarating gamble— the pain, but also the pleasure and fun of it.

BETH LEVINE, 1960

Kabuki, 1960
Silk satin, gilded wood, leather sole.

Kabuki shoes were evocative of wooden-soled shoes worn by traditional Japanese theater performers. Beth wanted to make a "floating" shoe, like an airplane for the foot.

Transparent shoes take all the worry out of dressing, and if you're going on a trip, think of the space it saves in your suitcase.

BETH LEVINE, *THE BOSTON GLOBE*, 1975

Cinderella Shoe, 1961
Clear vinyl with Lucite heel, silver kidskin details and lining.

Herbert asked Beth to make a clear heel without unsightly screws showing through. She achieved this feat with the help of her friend Sara Little Turnbull, who was working on adhesives for 3M at the time.

The Levines are known as the people who make shoes that other people say can't be made.

EXCERPT FROM FAMOUS-BARR ADVERTISEMENT, MARCH 1970

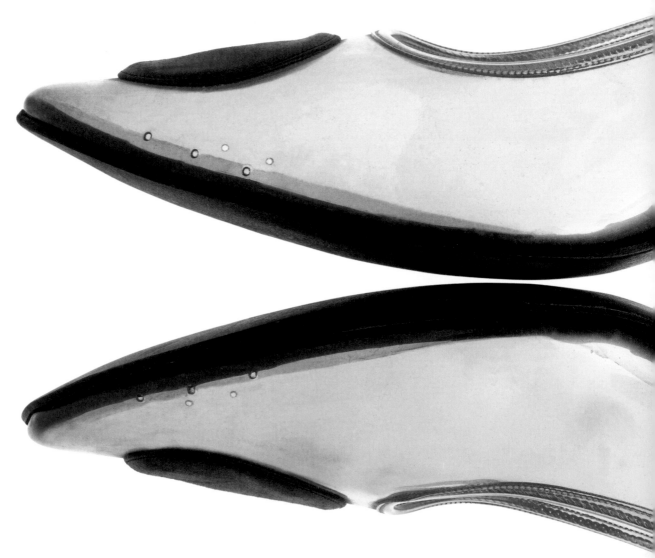

Title unknown, circa 1961
Vinylite, satin, and patent leather.

You get the
feeling these aren't
shoes at all, but works
of art, created by loving
hands, which in fact,
they are.

BARBARA LEVY, *ENVOY*, 1972

On a Roll, 1962
Turquoise velvet mule, sole of silver kidskin curled into tight spiral to form heel.

The Levines were always exploring new heel shapes. They were the first to introduce America to the "string bean" heel (later known as the "stiletto") and experimented with rolled and stacked leather, sculpted wood forms, and Lucite.

The heel must be absolutely flawless, as it carries the weight of the body.

BETH LEVINE, *MCCALL'S*, 1968

Safari, 1962
Leopard-printed hair on calfskin.

Alligator, 1957
Alligator.

Title unknown, 1962
Stenciled hair on calfskin in zebra pattern.

Known and appreciated as a luxury brand, the Herbert Levine line made heavy use of rare and exotic materials.

It's attuned to the thrust of the greatest architecture which adores the light . . . . The material is so full of movement it could propel itself into the twenty-first century!

BETH LEVINE, SPEAKING ABOUT VINYLITE, FALL 1969

Cowboy Boot, 1962
Polyvinyl chloride boot topstitched in beige cotton thread with suede tip and heel.

Made in America, steeped in surprise and whimsy, Levine shoes often expressed Americana themes, as illustrated by this pair of vinyl cowboy boots.

With everything
breaking down,
like the phone,
with so few
things real,
like the taste
of orange juice,
there's a longing
for quality.

BETH LEVINE, *NEW YORK POST*, DECEMBER 26, 1969

***Pavé Evening Shoe*, 1963**
Satin, black, gold, copper, and clear rhinestones in tiger pattern, leather sole and lining.

Beth collaborated with Steven Arpad, a rhinestone specialist working with Balenciaga in Paris, to make the first fully jeweled shoe. When Beth wore a pair of prototypes aboard a ship to Paris, buyers saw them and they became a sensation before she even returned home.

Chi Chi Boot, 1963
Black satin with beige, brown, and mustard silk-and-gilt thread in geometric pattern.

Superb fit, luxurious materials, and interesting shapes were the Levines' primary concerns. Thanks to Herbert's suppport, Beth had the freedom to use the finest (and most expensive) leathers and fabrics available, so the simplicity of the silhouette could dazzle, as in this pair of gold-embroidered ankle boots.

All my firm wants me to do is a Beth Levine this, or a Beth Levine that, and they don't want adaptations. They want copies.

ANONYMOUS SHOE DESIGNER TO *FOOTWEAR NEWS*, MARCH 10, 1975

Bianca, 1964
Kidskin pump with matching handbag.

Customers would often ask the Levines to make handbags to match their shoes. The Levines complied by supplying their materials to domestic manufacturers, in this case Koret.

Carol Channing has it, Arlene Francis has it, Lauren Bacall has it, Alicia Markova has it, Adele Simpson has it, Diahann Carroll has it, Mrs. Samuel Newhouse has it, Braniff stewardesses have it, Connie Stevens has it, Jill St. John has it, all the fashion editors have it, all the young models have it. WHAT DO THEY HAVE? BETH'S BOOT!

VIVIAN INFANTINO, *FOOTWEAR NEWS*, APRIL 20, 1967

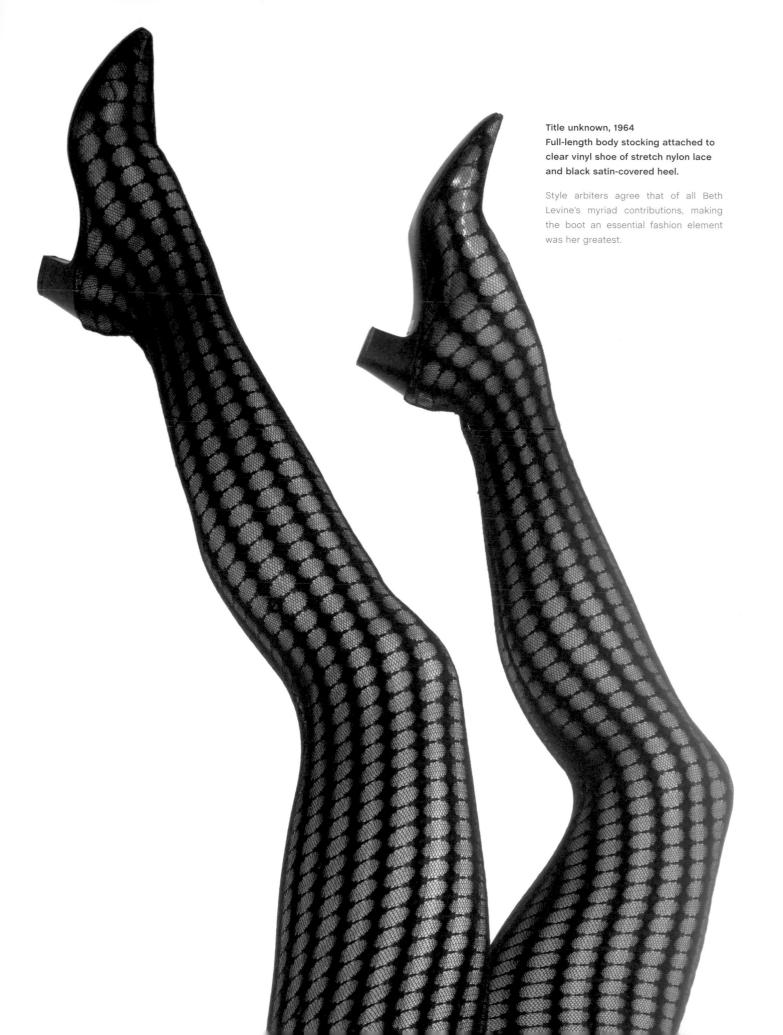

Title unknown, 1964
Full-length body stocking attached to clear vinyl shoe of stretch nylon lace and black satin-covered heel.

Style arbiters agree that of all Beth Levine's myriad contributions, making the boot an essential fashion element was her greatest.

Beth Levine was one of the truly great original designers that the United States ever produced.

VIC MARKIN, PRESIDENT, JOSEPH SALON SHOES

Bandana Evening Shoe, 1965
Red, black, and white silk satin pump with hand-glued jet and chalk beads. Fabric by Julian Tomchin.

A quintessentially American designer, Beth abhorred the prevailing tendency in the industry to imitate European designers. Her designs exemplified American ingenuity and used themes that were specific to the United States, like these beaded bandana shoes for evening wear.

Clothes must look unthought about, unplanned, as though it just happened somehow. It is very "out" to be "fashionably" dressed.

BETH LEVINE TO HELENE VERIN

Title unknown, circa 1965
Distressed leather boot with cotton
crewel work, back zipper.

These "shabby-chic" boots with frayed
edges are at least three decades ahead of
later designs that toyed with deconstructiv-
ism in fashion.

The wheel is an extension of the foot.

MARSHALL MCLUHAN, *THE MEDIUM IS THE MESSAGE*, 1967

Race Car Shoe, 1965
Patent leather, clear vinyl, glass studs, aluminum rings, kidskin lining, leather sole.

The Levines produced many versions of this shoe, originally designed for the wife of an Indianapolis 500 driver, featuring a windshield and headlights. It was featured in the 1967 film *Sole Art*, produced for the Coty Awards, as well as in a full-page editorial spread in *Harper's Bazaar* in March 1967.

Why does everything have to be for everybody?

BETH LEVINE

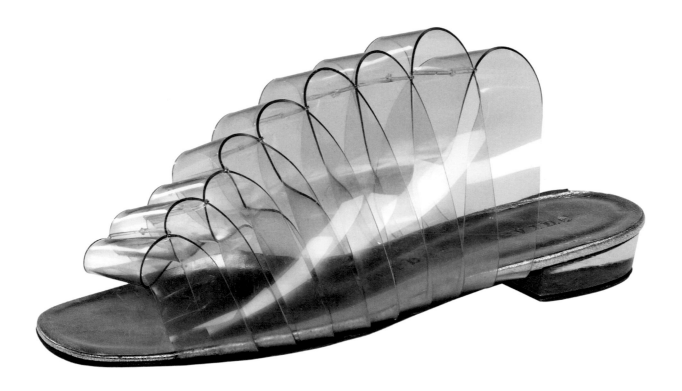

Ribbon Candy, 1965
**Vinylite strips twisted to form three-dimensional
loops for a wave effect, Lucite heel, silver
kidskin insole.**

Trio, circa 1965
**Pearlized leather with silver piping, velvet and satin
details at throat, heel, and toe.**

Forever mixing luxurious fabrics, Beth had this regal take
on the classic Chanel tip.

EVERYONE has a story to tell about his or her shoes.

BETH LEVINE

"It hasn't
been done before"
and "keeping shoes in
the conservative corner"
are industry maxims I
don't understand.

HERBERT LEVINE

***Jockey Boot,* 1965**
Leather.

Beth and Herb were horseracing aficionados. They owned race-horses and visited racetracks on their worldwide travels. This boot shows off different racing colors. It's also reminiscent of the work of the artist Joan Miró.

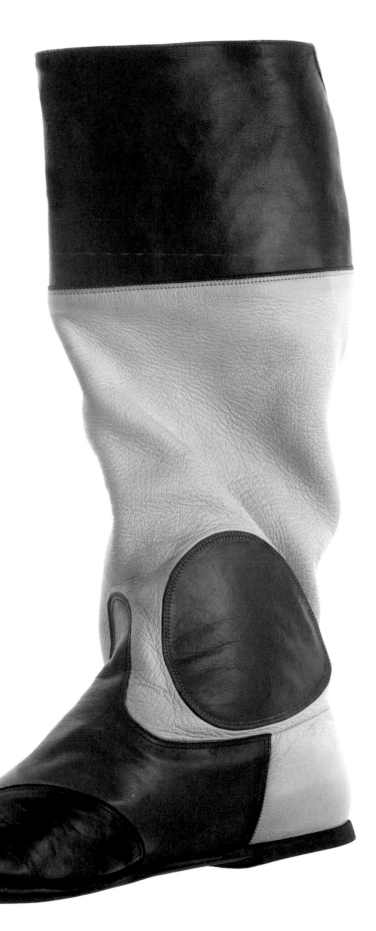

Why does everyone want to be first, second?

RUTHIE BALLIN, BETH LEVINE'S SISTER AND IN-HOUSE SHOE
DESIGNER FOR SAKS FIFTH AVENUE

Barefoot in the Grass, 1966
Wood, paint, plastic, and AstroTurf.

Beth, who referred to herself as a "farmer's daughter," constantly
used nature as a source of inspiration. This thong is from a series
of sandals utilizing AstroTurf as an insole, so, as she explained, "the
grass goes with you."

Boots pare down the legs to give the illusion of thinness. They promise to make legs more sensational than when garbed in stockings, or worse, nothing.

BETH LEVINE, *THE BOSTON GLOBE*, SEPTEMBER 25, 1970

Marlene Boot, 1966
Thigh-high stretch nylon boot, elastic band at top, back-of-knee dart; came with its own Herbert Levine garter belt.

Named for the famous legs of Marlene Dietrich, these iconic boots helped win the Levines their first Coty Award in 1967.

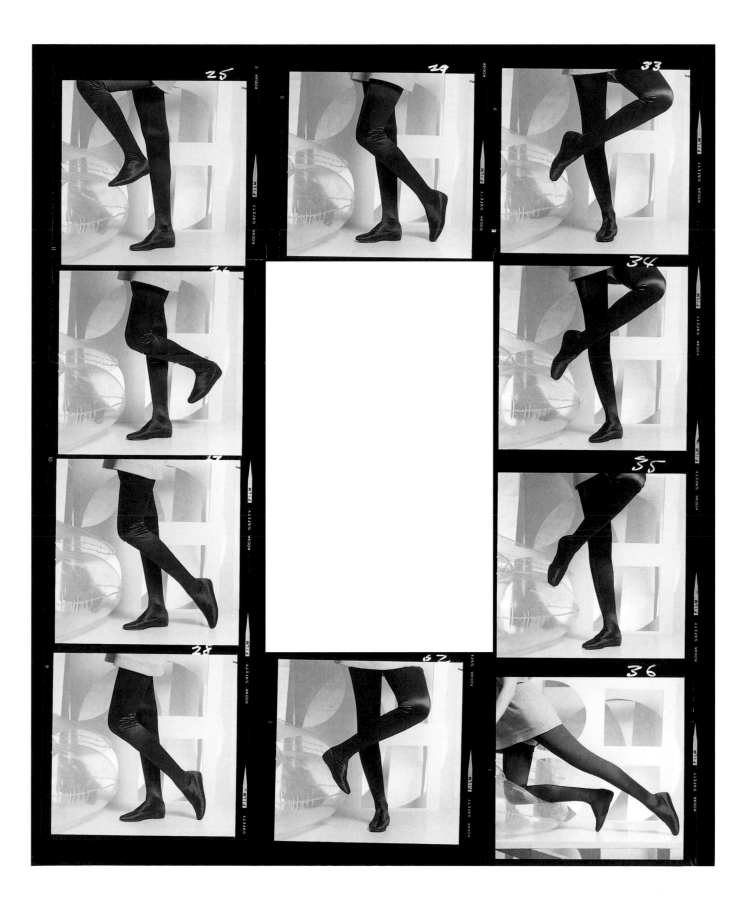

Before stretch boots, a skinny-legged woman in boots looked like a rooster wearing socks.

BETH LEVINE, *EASTON EXPRESS*, DECEMBER 3, 1971

Title unkown, 1967
Nylon with rhinestone buckle.

Skin-tight, form-fitting boots remain Beth's most important contribution to fashion. The fashion spread, like many of Beth's other innovations, by word of mouth. Worn by women of all ages, it was widely copied.

Paper shoes? Oh that was just done for fun! Sometimes shoes are just fantasies, really.

BETH LEVINE, BATA SHOE MUSEUM INTERVIEW, 1995

Paper Twist, 1967
Laminated paper strips, composition soles, oval heel.

Beth called these paper shoes "just right for your at-home costumes."

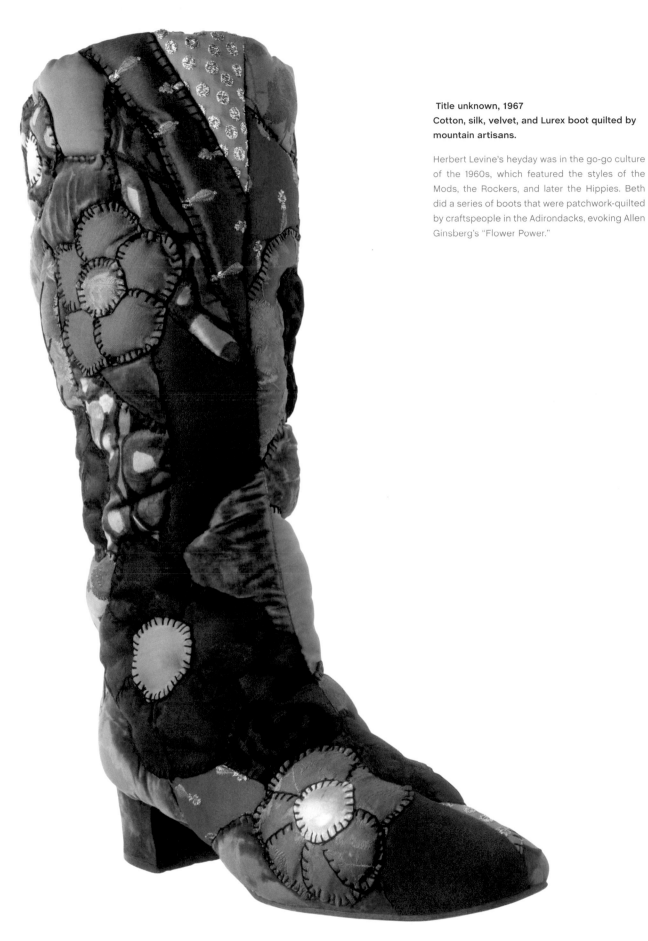

Title unknown, 1967
Cotton, silk, velvet, and Lurex boot quilted by mountain artisans.

Herbert Levine's heyday was in the go-go culture of the 1960s, which featured the styles of the Mods, the Rockers, and later the Hippies. Beth did a series of boots that were patchwork-quilted by craftspeople in the Adirondacks, evoking Allen Ginsberg's "Flower Power."

The Levines produced a line of avant-garde footwear that by its fantasy, inventiveness, humour, delicacy, sculptural balance and innovative use of materials can delight the eye and engage the spirit as only art can.

JUDY STOFFMAN, *THE TORONTO STAR*, JULY 27, 2000

Champion, 1968
Pearlized leather pump with milk-glass studded tongue extending from sole to high vamp.

Beth made several versions of this comfortable walking shoe, which has a novel open-yet-closed toe style.

Blending technology and design is a must!

BETH LEVINE, 1979 SPEECH TO THE DEPARTMENT OF COMMERCE

Moon Boot, 1968
Slipper with wraparound sole and vamp
of reflective silver vinyl, dot-printed suede,
interior wooden wedge.

A series of space-age boots and shoes were cre-
ated to celebrate the first landing on the moon.
Hiro photographed this series for a full page in
Harper's Bazaar.

Plastic shoes have some psychological value, they give some of that gay la-di-da feeling that some women used to get from high heels.

BETH LEVINE TO EUGENIA SHEPPARD, *NEW YORK HERALD TRIBUNE*, MARCH 23, 1966

Top: *Rhinestone Toes*, 1966
Vinylite, kidskin, rhinestones.

Middle: *Disco Pump*, date unknown
Vinyl, kidskin.

Bottom: *Spirit Step-In*, 1969
Vinylite, Macassar snakeskin.

Beth embraced transparent vinyl in the early 1950s, and went on to make clear vinyl sandals, loafers, pumps, and even cowboy boots.

Super Step-In, 1969
Black-on-tan cheetah-pattern hair on calfskin, high-throat pump with brass buckle.

Animal and reptile prints (such as alligator, python, and snakeskin) were a recurring theme throughout Beth's work. She made shoes and boots in leopard, cheetah, and zebra prints, and in real or faux leathers and furs.

Comfort IS fashionable!

BETH LEVINE

Americans love flashbacks. Now that Americans feel insecure about our country, there's that feeling of wanting to recapture "the good old days."

BETH LEVINE TO MARIAN CHRISTY, *BOSTON EVENING GLOBE,* APRIL 7, 1972

Title unknown, circa 1970
Silk satin with metallic ornament.

Red, white, and blue: one of Beth's trademarks is shown here in a wonderful evening pump, American through and through.

Why am I doing flats? You want to move along these days, you're not going to loll around like in a 1930s movie.

BETH LEVINE, *THE NEW YORK TIMES*, FEBRUARY 23, 1970

Summer Boot, 1970
Wool felt, embossed calfskin, sueded snakeskin, paper, and rubber.

These boots were prototypes and appeared in *Harper's Bazaar* in June 1970, photographed by Hiro. Always shuffling the traditional seasons in footwear fashions, Beth experimented here with a colorful boot for the summer.

These boots are made for walkin' And that's just what they'll do.

One of these days these boots are gonna walk all over you.

NANCY SINATRA, "THESE BOOTS ARE MADE FOR WALKIN'"

Chinese Lantern, 1970
Green suede boot, with red, rust,
purple, navy, and beige suede
vertical strips.

Referencing slashed shoes and
boots from the Renaissance, these
sumptuous boots reveal the leg
through seductive slits.

The only consistency in fashion is change.

HALSTON

City Sandal, 1970
**Suede, leather, gold-tone studs on
platform sandal.**

There were countless variations on the
platform sandal in the early 1970s. Beth
used every conceivable material and
color for her comfortable city sandals.

Women adored Levine boots. They knew they were in exquisite materials, made to last, fashion-right, and sinfully comfortable.

VIVIAN INFANTINO, MARCH 10, 1975

Carriage Boot, 1970
Printed rayon challis in paisley pattern, inside zipper, laced front with gold-tone grommets and ends.

The Levines made this boot in a myriad of combinations of leather, stretch patent leather, and printed and embroidered fabrics. Beth's designs were remarkable for their sense of spontaneity. Unlike fabricating overseas, producing shoes where she lived afforded Beth the pleasure of finding novel materials and creating a prototype from them the same day.

Shoes talk to you. In troubled times you equate shoes with security. The feeling of something on your feet bolsters your sense of well-being.

BETH LEVINE, FALL 1970 PRESS RELEASE (MURIEL DURAND)

Lovely Line, 1971
Hand-painted suede pump.

The motifs on these pumps, reminiscent of Aztec symbols, are yet another example of the many cultural influences on Beth's work.

Butterfly Boot, 1971
Silk and linen embroidered knee-high boot.

Beth designed these whimsical boots—inspired by her childhood on a dairy farm on Long Island—with embroidered butterflies. Insects and butterflies were important motifs in twentieth-century art and fashion, and were used extensively by Salvador Dali, Andy Warhol, and Elsa Schiaparelli.

We travel, fly, move, jump!

BETH LEVINE'S RATIONALE FOR BOOTS, *NEW YORK POST*, DECEMBER 26, 1969

Boots moved into prominence the same time The Pill did. Both were symbols of a woman's new freedom and emancipation.

BETH LEVINE, *THE BOSTON GLOBE*, JUNE 2, 1970

Wedge Boot, 1971
Printed leather, crepe sole.

Always in search of comfort in footwear, Beth adored the flexibility of crepe soles and used this construction in many of her styles. Beth noted, "Crepe is like a pullover, a sweater, it's friendly. It doesn't intrude, you can put it on everyday and it has that little bit of bounce" (*Footwear News*, July 27, 1972). Both Geoffrey Beene and Halston used these boots in their runway shows.

And you'll stand out
in buttons and bows…

"PARADE SONG," SUNG BY BOB HOPE IN *PALEFACE*, 1948

Assortment of ornaments

Joseph Acuti, who worked in the Levine factory, said, "No one's bows were prettier." Joseph was the nephew of Tony Acuti, after whom the Levines named their "Tony the Shoemaker" label.

Clockwise from top left:
Red Dot, 1954; *Spinnaker*,
1972; *White Grapes*, 1959;
Title unknown, 1961; Title
unknown, circa 1956; *Drum
Heel*, 1971; Title and date
unknown; *Hustler Heel*, 1966

REFERENCES

notes

[1] Sarah Ferguson, "Shoe-In," *Elle*, March 1992, 248.

[2] Edna Woolman Chase and Ilka Chase, *Always in Vogue* (New York: Doubleday & Co.), 1954.

[3] Herbert Levine, "Senior Citizen or Señor Citizen" (unpublished manuscript).

[4] Coincidentally, I designed shoes in the same factory in the late 1970s when it was called Scalise Stitching.

[5] Herbert Levine, "Senior Citizen or Señor Citizen."

[6] Beth Levine, interview by the author, September 25, 2004.

[7] Ibid.

[8] Herbert Levine, interview by Mildred Finger, November 23, 1982.

[9] Arthur Schwartz, interview by the author, October 17, 2007.

[10] Barbara Levy, "Beth Levine: America's First Lady of Shoe Design," *Envoy*, Spring 1972.

[11] Herbert Levine, "Senior Citizen or Señor Citizen."

[12] Ibid.

[13] Beth Levine, interview by Mildred Finger, November 23, 1982.

[14] Joseph Acuti, interview by the author, February 16, 2008.

[15] Herbert Levine, "Senior Citizen or Señor Citizen."

[16] Ibid.

[17] Beth Levine, interview by the author, August 22, 2006.

[18] Herbert Levine, interview by Mildred Finger, November 23, 1982.

[19] Beth Levine, interview by the author, June 22, 2005.

[20] *Glamour*, September 1, 1953, 183

[21] Beth Levine, interview by the author, September 11, 2006.

[22] When the Levines closed their factory in 1976, Sara Little Turnbull bought everything in her size (the same as Beth's, 4B). Because of this, Sara's collection, kept in archival boxes, boasts six hundred pairs in all and is one of the most interesting in existence.

[23] Beth Levine, interview by Nancy Pollock, January 4, 2000.

[24] Ibid.

[25] Ibid.

[26] Eleanor Lambert, Herbert Levine press release, Fall 1967.

[27] Vivian Infantino, "The Sleeper," *Footwear News*, July 27, 1972, 8.

[28] Eugenia Sheppard, "Shoes, Like Sundials, Tell Time," *Hartford Courant*, August 22, 1967, 11.

[29] Muriel Durand, Herbert Levine press release, December 2, 1970.

[30] Elizabeth Semmelhack, interview by the author, February 21, 2007.

[31] Beth Levine, interview by the author, May 23, 2004.

[32] Vivian Infantino, "The Real Skinny: The Super-tight Knee-high Boot Is on Fashionistas' Minds Once Again," *Footwear News*, May 29, 2000.

[33] Ferguson, "Shoe-In," 250.

[34] The shoes are in the Smithsonian Collection in Washington, D.C., and The Bata Shoe Museum.

[35] Beth Levine, interview by the author, January 14, 2005.

[36] Beth Levine, interview by Nancy Pollock, January 4, 2000.

[37] Beth Levine, interview by the author, August 22, 2006.

[38] Beth Levine, speech before the Department of Commerce, June 2, 1978.

[39] Herbert Levine, interview by Mildred Finger, November 23, 1982.

[40] Ibid.

[41] Elizabeth Semmelhack, interview by the author, February 21, 2007.

exhibitions

"Adele Simpson: American Fashion Designer," The Bruce Museum, Greenwich, Connecticut, 1997

"Arbiters of Style: Women at the Forefront of Fashion," The Museum at the Fashion Institute of Technology, 2008

The Costume Institute at the Metropolitan Museum of Art, New York, 1976

"Dance!" The Bata Shoe Museum, Toronto, 1997–99

"Fifty Years of American Women in Fashion," The Museum at the Fashion Institute of Technology, New York, 1981

"Footwear Exhibition," Marsil Museum, St. Lambert, Quebec

"The Height of Fashion," St. Clair Shopping Mall, Toronto, 1994

HemisFair, Women's Pavilion, San Antonio, 1968

"Herbert and Beth Levine: An American Pair," The Bata Shoe Museum, Toronto, and Headley-Whitney Museum, Lexington, Kentucky, 2000

"Icons of Elegance," The Bata Shoe Museum, Toronto, 2005–06

"If the Shoe Fits," San Francisco Museum of Fine Arts, 1997

"Pop Goes the Plastic," Atlanta International Museum of Art, and Katonah Museum of Art, Katonah, New York, 1998

"Shoes: A Lexicon of Style," The Museum at the Fashion Institute of Technology, New York, 1999

"Stepping Out," Powerhouse Museum, Sydney, Australia, 2006

"Beth Levine: From Farm to Fashion," Bellport-Brookhaven Historical Society, New York, 2007

awards

Coty American Fashion Critics' Award, 1973

Coty American Fashion Critics' Award, 1967

Kaufmann's of Pittsburgh Fashion Award, 1963

Leather Industries of America, American Shoe Designer Award, 1961

Neiman Marcus Award for Distinguished Service in Fashion, 1954

collections

The Bata Shoe Museum, Toronto, Canada

The Costume Institute at the Metropolitan Museum of Art, New York

Deutsches Ledermuseum Schuhmuseum, Offenbach, Germany

Dutch Leather and Shoe Museum, Waalwijk, The Netherlands

Kyoto Costume Institute, Kyoto, Japan

The Montreal Museum of Fine Arts, Quebec, Canada

The Museum at the Fashion Institute of Technology, New York

Museum of the City of New York, New York

National Museum of History, Smithsonian Collection, Washington, D.C.

Northampton Museum and Art Gallery, Northampton, England

Powerhouse Museum, Sydney, Australia

Sara Little Turnbull Archives, Seattle, Washington

Shoe-Icons, Moscow, Russia

Texas Fashion Collection, University of North Texas School of Visual Arts, Denton, Texas

bibliography

BOOKS AND ARTICLES

Adams, Carol. "Latest Shoe Designs Being Shown in City." *Oregon Journal*, February 7, 1955.

Allen, Jane. "Printed Leathers Arrive." *The Oregonian*, February 7, 1955.

"The American Shoe Experience: A Snapshot of People and Places from a Bygone Era." *Footwear News*, April 17, 1995.

Anniss, Elisa. "Designing Superstars." *Footwear News*, May 26, 1997.

Avedon, Richard, ed. *Hiro: Photographs*. Boston: Little, Brown, & Co., 1999.

"Award Winners." *Dallas Times Herald*, August 15, 1954.

Babette. "Fabulous Shoes Are New Inside and Out." *Los Angeles Examiner*, December 13, 1956.

Baker, Ruth Holman. "Face It! High Heels Are Sexy." *Dallas Morning News*, December 6, 1956.

"The Belt Way." *New York Times*, August 24, 1997.

Bender, Marilyn. "This Year Even the Shoe Designers Are Confused." *New York Times*, February 20, 1970.

Bernard, Barbara. "Fashion Has Its Foot in Many Doors." *Holyoke Transcript-Telegram*, December 12, 1971.

Berry, Heidi L. "Searching for the Perfect Costume: As Auctioneers Offer Old Couture, Knowing Eyes Focus on the Seams." *Washington Post*, September 23, 1993.

"Beth Levine." *Boutique Magazine*, March 1971.

"Beth Levine, Designer/Owner, Herbert Levine, Inc." *Footwear News*, April 8, 1974.

"Beth's Coty Award Is Good as Gold!" *Indianapolis Star*, sec. 6, 9.

Bjorkman, Carol. "Carol Says." *Women's Wear Daily*, July 24, 1963.

Capelaci, Sylvi. "Beads, Buckles, and Bows: Four Hundred Years of Embellished Footwear." *Ottawa Sun*, October 4, 2004.

———. "Design Intervention." *Calgary Sun*, October 24, 2004.

Carmichael, Celia. "L'Enfant Terrible: Five Minutes with Bad Boy Benoît Méléard." *Footwear News*, July 23, 2001.

Carofano, Jennifer. "Closet Case: Five Minutes in the Wardrobe and Creative Mind of Bettye Muller." *Footwear News*, April 30, 2001.

Carofano, Jennifer, Matt DeMazza, Stephen Dowdell, Kristin Larson, Jennifer Mooney, Jennifer Owens, Brian Russak, Sarah Taylor, and Natalie Zmuda. "Lasting Impressions." *Women's Wear Daily*, March 15, 2004.

Chase, Edna Woolman, and Ilke Chase. *Always in Vogue*. New York: Doubleday & Co., 1954.

Christy, Marian. "Fashion Comes Alive with Its Boots On." *Boston Globe*, September 25, 1970.

———. *Oakland Tribune,* February 19, 1975.

———. *San Mateo County Times,* December 19, 1973.

———. "Shoes: A Pair of Psychologies." *Boston Evening Globe,* April 7, 1972.

———. "A Society Is Revealed By Its Women's Shoes?" *Boston Evening Globe*, June 2, 1970.

C.S. "With Beth, The Shoe Fits." *San Francisco Examiner*, October 28, 1971.

Dale, D. "Never Again the Spiked Heel!" *Brockton Daily Enterprise*, November 8, 1968.

DeCaro, Frank. "A Night Out With: Michael Vollbracht." *New York Times*, November 5, 2000.

"Design Team Has Shoe Museum at Its Feet." *Toronto Star*, June 10, 1999.

DiNoto, Andrea. *Art Plastic: Designed for Living*. New York: Abbeville Press, 1984.

Duka, John. "Notes on Fashion." *New York Times*, October 13, 1981.

———. "76 Leading Women of Fashion Honored at Show." *New York Times*, September 21, 1981.

"East Is East and West Is West, And the Twain Shall Meet at Levine." *Footwear News*, July 8, 1955.

Eidelberg, Martin, ed. *Designed for Delight: Alternative Aspects of Twentieth Century Decorative Arts*. New York: Flammarion, 1997.

"Fame, Fortune, and Footwear." *Footwear News*, December 9, 2002.

"Farmer's Daughter to Win Award for Shoe Fashion Trends." *Journal & Constitution*, Atlanta, Georgia, August 22, 1954.

The Fashion Book. London: Phaidon, 1988.

"Fashion: Boots, Boots, Boots." *Time*, January 3, 1964.

Ferguson, Sarah. "Shoe-In." *Elle*, March 1998.

"The FN 50 — Industry Leaders: 1940–1995; Supplement; 50-Year Retrospective of Shoe Industry." *Footwear News*, October 16, 1995.

"Footnotes." *Toronto Sun*, Fashion Section, June 1, 1999.

Forgang, Isabel. "At Your Service." *Daily News*, February 17, 1970.

"From Far-Flung Distances." *Dallas Times Herald*, Section 3 Cover, September 7, 1954.

"Get Your Kicks at Fascinating Footwear Display." *Charlotte Observer*, April 8, 2001.

"Goddesses Reign." *Footwear News*, April 28, 2003.

Goldberg, Gail. "It's a Shoe World; Shoe Lovers Can Finally Fulfill Their Wanderlust with a Trip to FN's Top Seven Footwear Destinations." *Footwear News*, February 26, 2001.

Goldman, Judith. *Windows at Tiffany's: The Art of Gene Moore*. New York: Harry N. Abrams, 1980.

Graham, Rubye. "New Look in Shoes." *Philadelphia Inquirer*, March 31, 1964.

The Great American Foot. New York: The Museum of Contemporary Crafts of the American Crafts Council, 1978.

Greco, Susan L. "The First Lady of Shoe Design." *Long Island Advance*, October 11, 2006.

Harton, Rose Margaret. "Spring Shoes Put Their Best Food Forward." *Dallas Morning News*, January 20, 1974.

"He Said, She Said—Plenty of Shoes People Have Been Talking About During the Last 10 Decades—And FN Has Been Listening." *Footwear News*, April 26, 1999.

"Herbert and Beth Levine Design Shoes." *Houston Post*, January 28, 1969.

"Herbert Levine: Designed Award-Winning Shoes." *Los Angeles Times*, August 14, 1991.

Hessen, Wendy. "Scouting the Trade Shows: Accessories Circuit and Fashion Accessories Expo, 1997." *Women's Wear Daily*, May 12, 1997.

"History Lesson: A Look Back—From Fiamma Ferragamo to Sigerson Morrison, The Wild Pair to Scoop; Footwear News Reviews the Past 19 Years of Annual Achievement Awards." *Footwear News*, December 6, 2004.

"Husband-Wife Shoe-Design Team Rated as Industry's 6th Largest." *Dallas Morning News*, August 22, 1954.

Hyde, Nina S. "Fashion Notes." *Washington Post*, June 25, 1978.

"Inaugural Fashions Announced." *Sheboygan Press,* January 18, 1973.

Infantino, Vivian. "Coffee Table Tales: From Blahnik's Biography to Mizrahi's Comics, All I Want for Christmas Are Books, Books, Books." *Footwear News*, December 11, 2000.

———. "Dare to Bare Those Heels These Days; Half a Shoe is Better Than a Whole." *Footwear News*, February 3, 2003.

———. "Dateline New York." *Footwear News*, April 22, 1991.

———. "Fashion Viewpoint." *Footwear News*, July 7, 1967.

———. "Fashion Viewpoint." *Footwear News*, July 27, 1972.

———. "Fashion Viewpoint." *Footwear News*, March 10, 1975.

———. "Fashion Viewpoints 1960–1995." *Footwear News*, April 17, 1995.

———. "Let it Rain: Rainy Day Footwear." *Footwear News*, May 3, 1993.

———. "Museum Watch: The Met's Costume Institute Is Preserving the Past and Looking to the Future." *Footwear News*, August 10, 1998.

———. "The Non-Shoe: The Shoe Is Dead, Long Live the Shoe." *Footwear News*, November 30, 1998.

———. "Only Yesterday: Fashion Is Coming Out of the Closet." *Footwear News*, October 11, 1993.

———. "The Real Skinny: The Super-tight Knee-high Boot Is on Fashionistas' Minds Once Again." *Footwear News*, May 29, 2000.

———. "Viewpoints: A Stroll down Memory Lane Takes Us from High-Button Shoes to Stilettos, with Stops at Boots, Big Bottoms and Black Pumps Along the Way." *Footwear News*, April 26, 1999.

———. "What's Comfort Got to Do with It? High Thin Heels Made a Comeback." *Footwear News*, July 5, 1993.

———. "Who's On First? First Ladies and Their Fashion Styles." *Footwear News*, January 18, 1993.

———. "Women's Fashion: 1945–1985." *Footwear News*, October 6, 1985.

"The Innovators: Designs Aside, These Are the Preeminent Minds and Personalities that Have Spearheaded the Footwear Industry." *Footwear News*, April 17, 1995.

Kablean, Carrie. "Foot Fetish." *Weekend Australian*, November 22, 1997.

Kay, Ronald, and Susan Smith. "Headhunter Recalls When Trophies Were Elusive: Perspectives from Footwear Industry Executives." *Footwear News*, February 12, 1990.

Kelly, Carolyn. "A Museum with More Shoes than Imelda Marcos." *Austin American-Statesman*, January 23, 2000.

Klemesrud, Judy. "New Places to Shop If You're 25 to 35." *New York Times*, February 12, 1970.

Kyoto Costume Institute, ed. *Fashion: A History from the 18th to the 20th Century*. Cologne: Taschen, 2002.

Lambert, Eleanor. "Fashion Boots: The '70s Look." *Chicago Daily News*, November 4, 1970.

Larkin, Kathy. "High Fashion Kicks." *Daily News*, July 17, 1967.

———. "Shoes to Remember," *Daily News*, August 5, 1976.

Lawrence, Beverly Hall. "Polishing the Shoe's Image: A New York Author Celebrates Footwear Through the Ages." *Newsday*, April 3, 1997.

Lee, Sarah Tomerlin, ed. *American Fashion: The Life and Lines of Adrian, Mainbocher, McCardell, Norell, and Trigère*. New York: FIT—Quadrangle/ The New York Times Book Co., 1975.

Levine, Beth. "Relating Technology to the Marketplace." Speech presented at the Department of Commerce meeting and symposium on shoes in the United States, June 2, 1978.

"Levines Put Romance into Shoe Business." *Dallas Times Herald*, August 22, 1954.

"Levines to Win Acclaim for Shoe Designs." *Indianapolis Star*, August 22, 1954.

Levy, Barbara. "Beth Levine: America's First Lady of Shoe Design." *ENVOY*, Spring 1972.

Livingstone, Evelyn. "See-Thru Shoes Catching On." *Chicago Tribune*, May 3, 1966.

LoRusso, Maryann. "Recycling Style." *Footwear News*, April 26, 1999.

Mader, Edward, and Sonja Bata. "A Tour of The Bata Shoe Museum." Interview by Jacki Lyden. *All Things Considered*, NPR, February 24, 1996.

Marcus, Stanley. *Minding the Store, A Memoir*. Boston: Little, Brown, & Co., 1974.

"Marilyn Monroe, Buddy Holly Leave Their Footprints." *Times Colonist* (Victoria, British Columbia), April 16, 2003.

Martin, Richard, and Harold Koda. *Diana Vreeland: Immoderate Style*. New York: Metropolitan Museum of Art, 1993.

McAllister, Robert. "Counter Spy Measures Rise Sharply: Corporate Espionage in Shoe Industry." *Footwear News*, February 10, 1995.

McConathy, Dale, and Diana Vreeland. *Hollywood Costume*. New York: Harry N. Abrams, 1976.

McDowell, Colin. *Shoes: Fashion and Fantasy*. New York, Rizzoli, 1989.

McEwen, Mark, and Hattie Kauffman. "Jonathan Walford, Curator of The Bata Shoe Museum in Toronto, Displays Some of the Museum's Collection of Shoes from Various Historical Periods." *CBS This Morning*, December 5, 1997.

McKay, Dierdre. "Pflights of Pfancy: A Tribute to Andrea Pfister's Creative Passion." *Footwear News*, January 29, 1996.

McKay, John. "Podiatrist Bares His Soles for Footwear Fanciers." *Calgary Herald*, April 3, 2003.

Miller, Jerry. "How Do New Designers, Line Builders Emerge?" *Footwear News*, July 9, 1990.

———. "Pondering Women's Place in the Shoe Biz." *Footwear News*, December 2, 1991.

———. *The Wandering Shoe*. New York: My Goodfriends, c. 1984.

Mitchell, Louise, and Lindie Ward. *Stepping Out: Three Centuries of Shoes*. Sydney: Powerhouse Publishing, 1997.

Monahan, Iona. "Art Is Fashion and Fashion Is Art." *Ottawa Citizen*, July 2, 1997.

———. "Fashion Illusion: Where Dress and Décor Meet." *Gazette*, June 23, 1997.

Morris, Bernadine. "David Kidd, 68, Designer of Suits for Women." *New York Times*, September 23, 1981.

———. "A Designer Returns to Praise." *New York Times*, September 10, 1989.

———. "U.S. Shoe Companies Are Getting a Foot Back in the Door." *New York Times*, August 14, 1976.

Naunton, Ena. "Shoemaker Goes for Buckles and Bows." *Miami Herald*, November 11, 1966.

"Neiman Marcus Choice for 1954 Design Leadership." *Women's Wear Daily*, September 2, 1954.

"Neiman Marcus 1954 Award Winners." *New York Times*, August 16, 1954.

"Neiman Marcus Will Make Fashion Awards Sept. 6–7 for 17th Time." *Dallas Morning News*, August 15, 1954.

"Notes on Fashion." *New York Times*, May 25, 1982.

O'Hara, Jo Ellen. "The Cinderella Ball." *The Birmingham News*, February 10, 1974.

O'Keeffe, Linda. *Shoes: A Celebration of Pumps, Sandals, Slippers & More.* New York: Workman Publishing, 1996.

"Organdy Wedding for Tricia." *Post Crescent,* May 30, 1971.

Padgett, Tania. "Soles of an Artist." *Newsday,* June 11, 2007.

Pattison, Angela, and Nigel Cawthorne. *A Century of Shoes: Icons of Style in the 20th Century.* Edison: Chartwell Book, Inc., 1997.

Pedersen, Stephanie. *Shoes: What Every Woman Should Know.* Newton Abbot: David & Charles, 2005.

Portrait, Evelyn. "Shopping the Town." *Cue,* February 21, 1970.

Pratt, Lucy, and Linda Woolley. *Shoes.* London: V & A Publications, 1999.

Preston, Ruth. "Stepping Off the Platform." *New York Post*, Magazine section, April 17, 1973.

———. "Talk About Clothes: Local Talent." *New York Post,* February 17, 1967.

Reilly, Maureen. *Hot Shoes: 100 Years.* Atglen, Pennsylvania: Schiffer Publishing, Ltd., 1998.

Riello, Giorgio, and Peter McNeil. *Shoes: A History From Sandals to Sneakers.* Berg Publishers, 2006.

Rossi, William A. "High Heels, The Agony and the Ecstasy." *Footwear News,* November 1985.

"Rummaging in the Past Uncovers Forgotten Words." *Footwear News,* October 6, 1985.

"A Sampler of Celeb Shoes." *Edmonton Sun,* April 5, 2003.

Schiro, Anne-Marie. "Herbert Levine, 75, Manufacturer of High-Fashion Women's Shoes." *New York Times,* August 10, 1991.

Schneider-Levy, Barbara. "Remembering Viv: For Over 50 Years, Footwear News' Vivian Infantino Kept Shoes in the Fashion Spotlight." *Footwear News,* October 18, 2004.

Semmelhack, Elizabeth. *Icons of Elegance, The Most Influential Shoe Designers of the 20th Century.* Toronto: Bata Shoe Museum, 2005.

Sheppard, Eugenia. "Farewell to the Uglies." *New York Post,* September 12, 1973.

———. "Inside Fashion: Longer But Lovelier." *New York Post,* June 8, 1973.

———. "Longer Skirts, Lighter Shoes Delight Shoemakers." *Herald Tribune News Service,* March 23, 1966.

———. "Shoes, Like Sundials, Tell Time." *Hartford Courant,* August 22, 1967.

"Shoe Show: A Toronto Exhibition of Celebrity Footwear Ranges from Elvis's Boots to Marilyn's Red Stilettos." *London Free Press,* April 17, 2003.

"Shoe Struck: Podiatrist Heels to Shoe Museum." *Calgary Sun,* April 3, 2003.

"Shoes of the Stars: Foot Doctor Collects Celebrity Footwear." *Halifax Daily News,* April 3, 2003.

"Shop Talk." *Playbill*, Week of January 3, 1955.

Silverman, Dick. "Thinkpiece: As the Century Draws to a Close, It's Time to Acknowledge the Names and Faces that Will Blaze in the Industry's Memory Forever." *Footwear News*, April 26, 1999.

Simmons, Julia Anne. "Shoe Styles Changing Say New York Experts." *Birmingham Post-Herald*, August 20, 1956.

"Some of the Celebrity Footwear on Display for the Next Year at Toronto's Bata Shoe Museum, Partly from the Museum's Own Collection, Others on Loan from Dr. Harvey Miltchin." *Canadian Press Newswire*, April 2, 2003.

Stephen, Beverly. "A Shoe Designer Who Cares About Comfort." *San Francisco Chronicle*, October 27, 1971.

Stoffman, Judy. "Designer Shows Off Her Artistic Soles." *Toronto Star*, July 27, 2000.

Stuart, Dick. "Fashion East." *Manhattan East*, August 22, 1972.

Toppman, Lawrence. "If you Dig Shoes, Take Your Tootsies to Toronto." *Charlotte Observer*, April 24, 2001.

Trasko, Mary. *Heavenly Soles.* New York: Abbeville Press, 1989.

Verin, Helene. *Beth Levine: From Farm to Fashion.* Bellport, New York: Brookhaven Museum, 2007.

Walford, Jonathan. *The Seductive Shoe: Four Centuries of Fashion Footwear.* New York: Stewart, Tabori & Chang, 2007.

Warhol, Andy, and Pat Hackett, eds. *The Andy Warhol Diaries.* New York: Warner Books, 1989.

White, Jackie. "Designer Footwear Is a Shoo-in as Sculpture." *Kansas City Star*, October 15, 1998.

———. "Well-Heeled Art Designer Footwear Is a Shoo-in as Sculpture," *Kansas City Star*, October 11, 1998.

Whitehead, Doris W. "What's Afoot? Shoes Take Backward Glance." *Easton Express*, December 1, 1971.

Wilson, Eric. "Beth Levine, 'First Lady of Shoe Design,' Is Dead at 91." *New York Times,* September 23, 2006.

———. "Creating a Diversion: Michael Vollbracht Will Design an Exhibition Called 'Beads, Buckles and Bows' for The Bata Shoe Museum in Toronto." *Women's Wear Daily*, August 27, 2004.

Wilson, Louise. "Herbert & Beth Levine: Style-setters, Award-winners." *Courier Journal*, July 28, 1967.

EDITORIAL PHOTOGRAPHS

Avedon, Richard. *Harper's Bazaar*, January 1964, 99–101.

———. *Harper's Bazaar,* April 1965, 148.

———. *Vogue,* November 1, 1969, 145, 144.

———. *Vogue,* August 15, 1970, 61, 68.

———. *Vogue,* February 15, 1971, 120.

Bailey, David. *Vogue,* September 1, 1964, 160.

———. *Glamour,* September 1, 1967, 150–51.

———. *Vogue,* August 1, 1968, 109.

———. *Glamour,* October 1, 1968, 154.

———. *Vogue,* January 15, 1970, 143.

———. *Vogue,* August 1, 1970, 77, 81.

———. *Vogue,* September 1, 1970, 402.

Bourdin, Guy. *Harper's Bazaar,* April 1968, 136.

Connors, William. *Glamour,* August 1, 1969, 169.

Dixon, Mel. *Harper's Bazaar,* December 1970, 103, 105.

Gill, Leslie. *Harper's Bazaar,* September 1956, cover, 51.

———. *Harper's Bazaar,* February 1957, 137.

Greene, Milton H. *Life,* February 17, 1958.

Hiro. *Harper's Bazaar,* February 1961, 103.

———. *Harper's Bazaar,* January 1963, 108–9.

———. *Harper's Bazaar,* January 1964, 100–101.

———. *Harper's Bazaar,* June 1964, cover, 51, 60–61.

———. *Harper's Bazaar,* March 1966, cover.

———. *Harper's Bazaar,* June 1966, 72, 74.

———. *Harper's Bazaar,* July 1966, 64–66.

———. *Harper's Bazaar,* December 1966, 133–34.

———. *Harper's Bazaar,* March 1967, 26–27, 124–25.

———. *Harper's Bazaar,* May 1967, 125–26.

———. *Harper's Bazaar,* July 1967, 82, 84–85.

———. *Harper's Bazaar,* September 1967, 304, 312.

———. *Harper's Bazaar,* July 1969, 64.

———. *Harper's Bazaar,* August 1969, 108–9.

———. *Harper's Bazaar,* June 1970, 76.

Kane, Art. *Vogue,* August 15, 1964, 58.

———. *Vogue,* February 15, 1965, 130.

King, Bill. *Harper's Bazaar,* December 1969, 134–35.

———. *Harper's Bazaar,* July 1972, 58.

———. *Harper's Bazaar,* December 1972, 68.

Leombruno-Bodi. *Glamour,* December 1, 1953, cover.

Lichfield, Patrick. *Vogue,* August 1, 1969, 145.

Leiber, Saul. *Mademoiselle,* May 1952, 115.

———. *Life,* May 24, 1954, 117.

———. *Life,* January 21, 1957, 27.

———. *Life,* February 17, 1958, 63.

———. *Life,* September 24, 1965, 62.

———. *Look,* August 8, 1967, 50.

———. *Harper's Bazaar,* September 1967, 378–79.

Matter, Herbert. *Vogue,* August 15, 1953, 19, 94.

———. *McCall's,* November 1968.

Mili, Gjon. *Life,* January 18, 1950.

Moore, James. *Harper's Bazaar,* December 1969, 176.

Newton, Helmut. *Vogue,* October 1, 1964, 179.

———. *Vogue,* January 1973, 158, 160.

Parkinson, Norman. *Vogue,* August 15, 1968, 106, 111.

Penati, Gianni. *Vogue,* November 1, 1969, 156.

Penn, Irving. *Vogue,* January 1, 1965, 87.

———. *Vogue,* September 1, 1967, 309.

———. *Vogue,* September 1, 1969, 401.

———. *Vogue,* November 1, 1969, 51–52, 153.

———. *Vogue,* September 1, 1970, 131, 326–27, 336, 340, 370.

———. *Vogue,* September 15, 1970, 326–27, 336, 340.

———. *Vogue,* January 15, 1971, 114–15.

———. *Vogue,* February 1, 1972, 138–39.

Petrucelli, Anthony. *Look,* April 15, 1969.

Puhlmann, Rico. *Glamour,* September 1, 1970, 180–81.

———. *Glamour,* November 1, 1971, 186–87.

Radkai, Karen. *Vogue,* November 1, 1955, 108.

Richardson. *Glamour,* January 1, 1970, 80.

Rizzo, Albert. *Harper's Bazaar,* March 1970, 191.

Rothstein, Arthur. *Look,* November 25, 1968, 70.

Rutledge, Richard. *Glamour,* September 1, 1953, 183.

Scavullo, Francesco. *Harper's Bazaar,* March 1966, 37.

———. *Harper's Bazaar,* July 1966, 90.

———. *Harper's Bazaar,* August 1966, 150–51, 336–37.

———. *Glamour,* March 1, 1967, 148.

———. *Harper's Bazaar,* November 1970, 135.

Silano. *Harper's Bazaar,* March 1967, 193.

Stern, Bert. *Vogue,* July 1, 1963, 80.

———. *Vogue,* November 1, 1964, 162–63, 183.

Stone, Bob. *Vogue,* August 15, 1972, 68.

Tieljens. *Glamour,* September 1953, 180.

———. *Vogue,* January 1, 1970, 131.

Waldeck, Alexis. *Vogue,* August 15, 1967, 118.

Zachariasen, J.P. *Glamour,* September 1, 1970, 158.

ADVERTISEMENTS

Neiman Marcus preview. *Dallas Times Herald,* September 5, 1954, sec. 1, 23.

"Wow" mule. *San Antonio Express,* December 9, 1954, 1D.

Patent leather halter-slings. *Houston Chronicle,* February 6, 1955.

Platinum calf. *Seattle Post-Intelligencer,* February 6, 1955.

Spring-o-lator. *Sunday Enterprise,* March 20, 1955.

Backless footwear fashions. *Birmingham News,* March 27, 1955, D-7.

Avocado. *Buffalo Courier Express,* March 30, 1955.

Herb and Beth at Frost Bros. *San Antonio Light,* February 1, 1956.

Frost Bros. fashion show. *San Antonio Express,* February 2, 1956.

Frost Bros. "Here in Person." *San Antonio Express,* February 2, 1956.

"Under Construction" presented. *Birmingham News,* August 19, 1956.

Saul Steinberg ad. *Harper's Bazaar,* March 1957.

"Holiday Glitter-toes." *Shreveport Times,* December 7, 1958.

Pale shoes. *Sun Times,* March 8, 1959.

Formal fantasies. *San Antonio Express*, December 2, 1962.

Wooden-soled sandal. *Chicago Daily Tribune*, January 4, 1963.

"Kabuki." *Tyler Courier-Times*, January 27, 1963.

Patent-leather pumps. *Seattle Post*, February 3, 1963.

Decorative pumps. *San Francisco Chronicle*, February 10, 1963.

Buckles from France. *Dallas Morning News*, October 24, 1966.

Patent pump. *Houston Post*, May 7, 1967.

"Good Queen Beth." *St. Louis Post-Dispatch*, March 31, 1970, 12A.

Beth's Bootery. *Harper's Bazaar,* September 1970, 8.

Beth's Bootery. *New York Times*, September 6, 1970, 29.

Boot. *Chicago Daily News*, November 4, 1970.

Saks Fifth Avenue. *Vogue.* February 15, 1971.

Ankle-strap shoes. *Times-Union*, September 21, 1971.

Evening boot. *New York Times*, November 29, 1971, 4.

Stocking boot. *Star-Ledger*, January 2, 1972, Sec. 2, p. 3.

Spoon platform. *Dallas Morning News*, March 12, 1973.

Strips on vinyl. *Minneapolis Star*, September 9, 1973.

Photo Credits

All photographs © 2009 David Hamsley unless otherwise noted. All footwear courtesy of the author unless otherwise noted.

2, 6, 74, 81, 154–55, 166–67, front cover: Schwartz & Benjamin, Inc. library, New York

16–18: © 2009 Bush Farm Museum

20: © 2009 Horst Estate, Staley-Wise Gallery, New York

27: © 2009 Philip Pearlstein

28, 29: © 2009 The Saul Steinberg Foundation/Artists Rights Society (ARS), New York

30: © 2009 Norman Parkinson Archive, London

32: © 2009 Gjon Mili, Time Life Pictures, Getty Images

34: Milton H. Greene © 2009 Joshua Greene

36, 37, 41, 42 (left), 82: Photographs courtesy Dutch Leather and Shoe Museum, Waalwijk, The Netherlands

42 (right), 46, 122, 129, 133, 143: Photographs courtesy The Bata Shoe Museum, Toronto, Canada

44: © 2009 Guy Bourdin Estate, Art + Commerce, New York

45: "Frank Sinatra and Daughter Nancy on TV," © 2009 Corbis

51: © 2009 Richard Avedon, The Richard Avedon Foundation, New York

55: © 2009 Bruce Weber

75, 123, 157, back cover (bottom): Photographs by Irving Solero, courtesy The Museum at FIT, Fashion Institute of Technology, New York

76, 149: New York Vintage, New York

83, 93, 117, 142, 151, 163: Courtesy Sara Little Center for Design Research, Seattle

85: Photographs courtesy DLM—Deutsches Ledermuseum Schuhmuseum, Offenbach, Germany

87, 90–91, 95, 105, 109, 110–11, 119, 153: Photographs courtesy The Costume Institute at The Metropolitan Museum of Art, New York

127, 139, 166: Ronald, Nancy, and Meghan Bush, Bayport

166–67 (drum heel): Angela Pontual, collection of Dorothy Louie, New York

Acknowledgments

This book is the culmination of six years of research and I am indebted to many. Thank you to:

Beth's remarkable family, who have invited me in with warmth and generosity: Jamie, Meghan, Ron and Nancy Bush, Nan Bush and Bruce Weber (along with Lisa Merkle and Nathan Kilcer at Little Bear, Inc.), Antonio and Tom Bryson, and Dorothy and Philip Pearlstein.

Sonja Bata and Harold Koda for their eloquent foreword and introduction, and to the staff of The Costume Institute of the Metropolitan Museum of Art and The Bata Shoe Museum for their support.

The Fashion Institute of Technology, including the director, Jeanne Golly, who encouraged my research, and Valerie Steele, Dr. Joyce Brown, and Irving Solero.

My tireless intern from the Fashion Institute of Technology, Vanessa Arlak, and to Clare Sauro for bringing us together.

Beth's many friends and admirers who contributed interviews and guidance, including Elizabeth Semmelhack, Joseph Acuti, Nancy Pollock, Arthur and Barbara Schwartz, Michael Vollbracht, Jeffrey Kalinski, Cathy Friedman, Kathryn Page, Azzedine Alaïa, Christian Louboutin, Manolo Blahnik, and Violet Gershonson.

My personal stellar friends/editors Elizabeth Field and Elaine Louie. B. J. Berti, who introduced me to my publisher, Leslie Stoker; editors, Rahel Lerner and Kate Norment; and designer, Alissa Faden.

Models Monique Connelly and Kate Piccin.

Inge Specht, the curator of the Dutch Shoe Museum, who had the idea for an exhibition that would coincide with the book publication, and to all the venues who are sponsoring the tour.

Paula Rees, whose priceless assistance with Sara Little Turnbull's collection and enduring understanding of this project remained a constant.

Above all, David Hamsley, my splendid photographer, who believed in and worked so diligently on this book, maintaining faith in an idea that may have never come to fruition.

Finally, my partner, Jim Burnham, and son, Ryder Ripps, for their patience and enduring support. And to the memories of my marvelous mother, Beatrice Verin, and mentor, Beth Levine, my inspirations.

Sailing Free

Swallow

Dash!

Profile

Bunny

Best Wishes

ON The Town

Our Beauty

Inside Story

Lover

Snap

Dandy

Little Tempest

PAGODA

Pago Pago

Free Verse

Fantastic Toe

OBI

Rag Doll

Pixie

Roberta

Captain
Kidd

Pussycat

Cupcake

THE CLOWN

Clue

Candlelight

Tack Room

Anchor

Inside
Story

New Craze

Get the Point

Plush

Garden of Eden

Quick Look

Glint
Sling

Second
Glance

Express

Lovely Pearl

Eyelash

As You Wish

Figaro

Two Button

Easy Does It

Stars In Your Eyes

Sophisticate

Perfect Setting

"Evensong"

Ever Lovin'

Coquette

Romantic Bow

Upbeat

Busy Life

Anytime

Four Bits

Pretty Foot

Ambassador

Sailing Free

Swallow

Dash!

Profile

Bunny

Best Wishes

ON The Town

Our Beauty

Lover

Inside Story

Snap

Dandy

Little Tempest

PAGODA

Pago Pago

Free Verse

Fantastic Toe

OBI

Rag Doll

Pixie

Sailing Free